The Project Management Book

The Project Management Book

Richard Newton

Harlow, England • London • New York • Boston • San Francisco • Toronto • Sydney
Auckland • Singapore • Hong Kong • Tokyo • Seoul • Taipei • New Delhi
Cape Town • São Paulo • Mexico City • Madrid • Amsterdam • Munich • Paris • Milan

PEARSON EDUCATION LIMITED
Edinburgh Gate
Harlow CM20 2JE
United Kingdom
Tel: +44 (0)1279 623623
Web: www.pearson.com/uk

COLEG SIR GAR GRAIG CAMPUS		
GR / 15 / 17 / 002		
BBfS		00065016

First published 2013 (print and elec

© Richard Newton 2013 (print and el

The right of Richard Newton to be id
asserted by him in accordance with th

Pearson Education is not responsible for the content of third-party internet sites.

ISBN: 978–0–273–78586–6 (print)
     978–0–273–78880–5 (PDF)
     978–0–273–78879–9 (ePub)

British Library Cataloguing-in-Publication Data
A catalogue record for the print edition is available from the British Library

Library of Congress Cataloging-in-Publication Data
Newton, Richard, 1964-
  The project management book / Richard Newton.
    pages cm
  Includes index.
  ISBN 978-0-273-78586-6 (pbk.)
  1. Project management. I. Title.
  HD69.P75N4947 2013
  658.4′04--dc23
                  2013005064

10 9 8 7 6 5 4 3
17 16 15

Cover design by David Carroll & Co.

Print edition typeset in 9pt Stone Serif by 3
Print edition printed and bound in Great Britain by Ashford Colour Press Ltd, Gosport, Hampshire

NOTE THAT ANY PAGE CROSS-REFERENCES REFER TO THE PRINT EDITION

Contents

About the author

Richard Newton is the author of *The Management Book*, winner of the 2013 CMI Management Book of the Year Award.

Richard has been managing projects for over 25 years, and for the last nine years has run his own specialist consultancy. Richard has a range of blue chip clients with whom he works worldwide and has worked across a range of sectors including the public sector, telecoms and media, mining, oil and gas, and financial services.

He is the author of ten books, including *The Project Manager: Mastering the Art of Delivery*.

Preface

I have written several books on project management, and every year many others are published. There is a rich seam of excellent project management writing (and unfortunately some very badly written books as well), so why another book?

I have written this for two reasons.

Firstly, as an evolving discipline, there is always something new to say about project management. I am not an armchair observer, but an active project manager. This book was written in evenings and weekends whilst being involved in two complex, leading-edge projects. I call myself a consultant, but my work is always as a full participant in a wide variety of projects. I love experiencing the project management discipline evolving to new challenges.

Secondly, I wanted to take advantage of a different format from the normal project management books. The format is issues based, enabling the reader to be able to dip into and read short, sharp advice on a specific issue or area of interest. I hope you read this book end to end, but it is not essential to do so to gain value from it.

This is a book about *projects* as much as *project management*. Project managers and project management sit at the heart of projects, but there is much more to projects than simply project management. Projects deliver outcomes that matter to people who have little or nothing to do with the project itself. Projects work in, are impacted by and impact environments, organisations, cultures and societies. Projects call upon and affect a wide variety of people.

I expect many of the readers of this book will be project managers, but it is not only for project managers. There is something here for anyone who is involved in, interested in, or wants to improve their capabilities in project management.

Any choice of contents is subjectively based on the author's experience and what he or she feels is important. A book cannot fit everything in. I have tried to cover an interesting array of issues facing projects – some are fundamental, others are challenges in specific contexts. I have had to prioritise as there is enough material for at least one more follow-up volume!

I have aimed for practical, readily usable advice that talks about the real issues facing projects. The focus is simple: how to run effective, efficient projects. You will find shortcuts to avoid some painful situations, and lessons that I and others have learned from trial and error.

Introduction

Project management is a great topic to write about, but it can seem hard to say anything new, simply because there is so much that has been written so far. However, it is an evolving discipline and like anything that is evolving, there is always novelty and innovation. This book combines essential proven fundamental project management concepts with newer thinking. The format aims to make the traditional advice more accessible than other books, and provides the newer guidance in easy-to-digest, bite-sized chunks.

The overall aim is to provide practical, comprehensible and value-adding advice to anyone who is interested in or involved in running projects. The advice is outcome orientated and can be put to immediate use. The book aims to be an everyday guide and a regular reference source.

The contents

The choice of this book's contents follows a plan. I have kept to the essential parts of project management, but look at them from unusual perspectives. I have combined fundamentals of getting projects right, with lessons and tips from experience – shortcuts to avoid pitfalls and seize opportunities, along with positioning of project management within the wider context in which it operates.

It is an eclectic mix, based on my experiences of running projects and my views of what is useful to know. Of course, there are limitations to what can be contained in one book, but I hope

I have prioritised on important topics. I have concentrated on practical advice for running projects – identifying real issues project teams face and how they can be overcome.

The structure

This book has been split into 10 parts, each of which focuses on an important project management theme. The parts are sub-divided into four sections, each containing one article. The articles are varied, but when combined provide a comprehensive view on the theme of the part. Although the articles build into a picture of project management, they are designed to stand alone. You can pick any section in any part of the book and read it as an individual piece of advice.

Each of the articles is short, and they are all structured in the same way. Each can easily be read in one very short sitting.

Who the book is for

The book has been designed for a wide readership – anyone interested in the reality of project management. Effective project managers, sponsors and team members need a strong grasp of project management theory. There are lots of great books, courses, websites and other resources for learning that theory. Instead this book is issues orientated. I asked myself, 'What issues occur on projects and how should they be resolved?' These issues can challenge anyone involved in a project, from the beginner to the more experienced project manager. The book covers a wide range of topics – starting with how to be able to explain some basic project concepts through to developing and improving a strong project management capability.

How to use the book

There are two ways to use this book. I hope you find both of them useful.

Read the book end-to-end to gain an overall picture of project management. There is a rough logical ordering to the parts, from part 1 starting with the basics and progressing to more sophisticated and complex issues. There are cross-references between the articles to help you build a flexible and many-sided view of management.

Alternatively, dip in and pick the articles that are most helpful to you. Each article is complete as a standalone read, and will help resolve real project issues in a practical way. Use the book as a reference source, reading articles as and when you want. Hopefully, you will come back to the book time and again – keeping it close by, on the desk from which you work when you are involved in projects.

Major project management terms are explained in the glossary at the end of this book and appear in italic when they are first met in each section.

one

The foundations

Each part of this book provides a set of advice related to one aspect of project management. There is a very rough progression in terms of expertise from one part to the next. This first part starts at the most simple level.

Exploring the subject of project management requires a basic level of knowledge. This basic knowledge relates to understanding the meaning and relevance of certain core concepts which are used all the time in discussing, explaining and justifying the discipline.

This part aims to explain the most basic and central terminology of project management. The primary readership for this part are those interested in projects for the first time. If you are an old hand at projects you may be tempted to skip this part. Instead try dipping in – you may surprise yourself and find something of interest!

I have tried to avoid the clichés of project management and find new ways to explain the central concepts: what is a project, what is project management, why do we need project managers and what do they do, and who are the community involved in projects?

Projects

What is this about and why is it important?

The concept of a project is fairly intuitive, but like many intuitive terms it is hard to define in a comprehensive and non-contentious way. It is always useful to understand the terms we use and to be able to explain them to other people. Unless the word 'project' is properly understood, the whole concept of *project management* will be at best flawed and at worst meaningless.

For many readers, this first section will be superfluous, but for those new to projects or anyone seeking to give definitions or describe projects to others, this is a good place to start.

Objectives

- To develop an understanding of projects
- To understand the difference between projects and other forms of endeavour

Common issues in achieving these objectives

→ Wide variation of dissimilar situations in which the term 'project' is applied

→ Difference between the everyday casual use of the term versus formal professional usage

The guide

Often, to understand a concept, it is more useful to explore how the term is used rather than to give a one-line dictionary definition. And so it is with the word 'project'. I find it most helpful to develop a picture of what projects are by describing their common characteristics.

One challenge is that the characteristics associated with projects vary depending on context. In this book, I am referring to projects in broad but specific circumstances – that is professional and business contexts, in which formal project management is being applied. In other contexts, for example in educational, creative and personal situations – the term may be used in the same way, but usually it is being used in a less formal manner.

There are nine characteristics which are common to projects in professional and business contexts. The way projects exhibit these characteristics varies hugely. By describing the characteristics it is possible to get a sense of what sorts of things projects are, but it is hard to give a simple universal picture that is applicable to all projects.

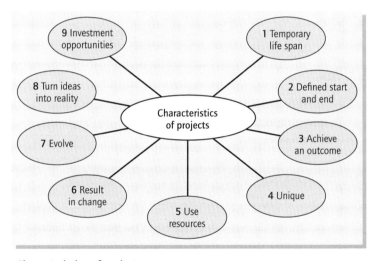

Characteristics of projects

It is not uncommon for commentators to describe some of these characteristics as black and white differentiating factors between projects and other forms of endeavours – most often operations. As will be explained below, whilst this difference may be typically true, it is not always so.

Let us look briefly at each of the characteristics.

Temporary life span

Projects are temporary. They exist for a limited period of time and then cease to be.

In theory projects can be very short. However, normally activities which only last a few hours or days would not be considered as projects, mainly because they are of insufficient complexity to justify applying project management. Projects typically last from weeks to months, but in some situations such as aerospace, defence and infrastructure may last years or even decades.

Projects are often compared to operations because they are temporary. In reality, in the era of continuous change, temporal limits can be just as short for operational activities as projects. It is true that typically projects last for a shorter period of time than operations. The real difference may be that projects are intended to be temporary, whereas a form of operations just ends up as temporary when a better way of doing things comes along.

Defined start and end

Projects do not just go from any point in time to any other, but have defined start and end points. The end point may be a date, but is more normally when some outcome is achieved. Often it is planned as a combination of the two as in 'the project will be complete on the 31st October when we have launched the new product'.

Achieve an outcome

Projects achieve an expected outcome, or at least successful ones do! This outcome may be defined in terms of a set of deliverables such as creating a new IT system or building, or in terms of meeting a set of planned *objectives*, such as improving operational performance.

Unique

Projects are unique. Every project varies to some extent in terms of outcomes, resources and context.

In reality, whilst each project is unique, there is a large degree of commonality between some projects. For example, a software development department in a business will run many projects. Lots of these will be similar to many others run in that department.

Use resources

Projects use or absorb resources. These are always time and human resources, and usually money. There is a wide variety of other resources that may be used: machines, tools, facilities and so forth.

This is an important characteristic of projects, as estimating, sourcing and managing the resources of a project is a significant part of a project manager's work. It is not a differentiating factor though, as pretty much anything done professionally – developing strategy, running operations, servicing customers, making sales, etc. – also uses resources.

Result in change

Projects always result in some form of change. When a project is complete, something must be different. If nothing is different the project has delivered nothing and has not been successful. The nature of this change is unique to each project, and the range of changes projects can achieve is vast. Compare projects which have resulted in the recent generations of consumer technology with those to build new transport infrastructure. Both have implications and create changes for large numbers of people, but the nature of that change is significantly different.

In contrast, operations typically do the same thing day in, day out, producing the same products and services for customers.

Evolve

Projects are normally subject to *progressive elaboration*. This is an important and somewhat subtle point. Progressive elaboration is a piece of project management terminology referring to the way understanding improves as projects progress, which in turn enables deeper detailing of plans, designs and approaches.

Projects are planned and designed as far as understanding allows at any point, and then progressively elaborated as the project progresses. A project plan shows lots of details for now and in the short term, and less detail further into the future. As time passes, and what was further in the future becomes close to now, the corresponding parts of the plan become increasingly detailed (see p. 39).

Turn ideas into reality

The purpose of any project is to make ideas reality. Sources of ideas may be strategies, new product concepts, technical designs and so forth. Projects are the motors of execution, starting with dreams, concepts, and images – and ending with deliverables, products and results. These ideas may be revolutionary – such as sending a manned rocket to Mars – or more mundane – such as refitting an office block.

Investment opportunities

Projects are usually investment opportunities. Many investments in business are made through projects. For this reason, the money spent on projects can often be capitalised. The nature of the investment and the justification for making the investment are defined in the project's business case.

Small projects may have informal business cases, but large projects may be some of the largest investments organisations make.

Project manager's checklist

- The term 'project' can be best understood by exploring the typical characteristics of projects

- Whilst there are characteristics common to all projects, the way projects exhibit these characteristics varies enormously

Project management

What is this about and why is it important?

The term *project management* is hard to define in a meaningful, non-contentious, concise and helpful way. There are many existing definitions, but they usually miss out important aspects, are too generic, convoluted, or give the wrong impression. Other definitions reflect writers' specific biases. This is possibly because project management is a broad and evolving concept. But we should try to find a shared definition if we are going to discuss the subject.

This section discusses the term project management. It is aimed both at novices and those practitioners experienced in project management. For the novice this is a straightforward introduction explaining the breadth of the concept. For the experienced practitioner, this section will help in those conversations in which you need to describe project management to someone else.

Objectives

- To provide an understanding of the term project management
- To develop an appreciation of the main components of project management

Common issues in achieving these objectives

→ Variations in understanding of the concept of project management

→ Different views of the boundaries of project management

The guide

One place to start to understand project management is with formal definitions. The various project management *bodies of knowledge (BoK)*, such as the *PMI* BoK and the *APM* BoK provide such definitions. Most project management books provide a description, as do relevant standards and dictionaries. I usually find these definitions either short and relatively unhelpful or constructed of convoluted and contrived sentences.

If I have to give a simple definition, I would say that project management is a way of reliably delivering a defined outcome. But this does not sufficiently differentiate project management from other approaches to getting things done.

The philosopher Wittgenstein argued that the meaning of words is in their use. When people use the words 'project management' they refer to a variety of inter-related concepts. The best way of thinking about project management is as an umbrella phrase, which can be broken down into inter-related concepts. Project management is made up of:

- **Goals:** project management is concerned with delivering outcomes in a predictable manner – for instance, delivery of *objectives*, or scoping within a predefined time, cost and to an agreed level of quality.

- **A way of thinking:** project management encourages a style of thinking. This thinking is structured, logical and directed towards goals. This thinking asks questions like: what is wanted, how do I get from where I am to where I want to be, what is the optimal balance of time, cost and quality?

- **Lifecycles:** project management is often presented in the form of *lifecycles*. A lifecycle is an overall way of structuring, thinking about, or discussing a project in a series of defined steps. A very simple example is a four-step lifecycle: initiate, plan, execute and close.

- **Practices and approaches:** project managers have a toolkit of practices, processes and tools used in defining, planning, monitoring and controlling projects. Examples include *risk* and issue *management*, estimation techniques and *stakeholder management*.

- **Methodologies:** many people think of a methodology when they think of project management. There are many debates about what precisely counts as a methodology – but essentially it is a guided way to deliver a project. It can be made up of lifecycles, processes, practices, role definitions, etc. Common project management methodologies are *PRINCE 2, critical chain* and *scrum.*

- **Styles of behaviour:** project management encourages and thrives when a certain style of behaviour is adopted: thinking ahead and planning; focusing on action, outcomes, *risk* and quality; and overcoming problems and obstacles in the way. When some people use the term project management, they mean adopting this style of behaviour.

- **A community of practitioners:** another way project management is used is to refer to the community of practitioners. This community includes project managers, and also project management officers, *programme managers* and *portfolio* managers.

Yet even this rich set of components does not cover everything that people refer to when they discuss project management. The precise boundary of what is included as project management varies. There are other topics that are certainly closely associated with it. These are:

- **Project management tools:** there are a range of tools, often in the form of templates and software packages which support project management. Included in this are planning and work management tools, such as *MS Project* and *Jira* and resource management tools, such as timesheet systems.

- **Project *governance*:** governance is the framework which links the project to the wider strategy and needs of a business. Typical aspects of governance are decision making and providing approvals.

- **Project *quality management*:** the activities to ensure that projects achieve the desired outcomes in the most appropriate way (considering standards, regulations, risk, etc.).

- **Project management offices**: *PMOs* are individuals or organisations who perform a range of administrative, governance, control and quality management activities on a project. The precise role varies from situation to situation. The PMO typically reduces the workload on project managers, enabling them to focus on the management and delivery of the project. A PMO may exist within a project or across multiple projects. The PMO may work for a project, or it may serve a body overseeing projects.

- **Programme** and **portfolio management**: these grew out of project management and have broadened the discipline enormously. The term project management refers both to the practice of managing projects, as well as the whole family of project, programme and portfolio management.

- **Other related practices**: there are many context-specific disciplines and practices which are required to deliver projects. These may not be project management but, depending on the context, project managers need to have a strong familiarity with them: for example, business analysis in IT projects or contract and sub-contractor management in construction projects. These are not really part of project management, but are closely associated with it by project managers working in specific industrial sectors or functional domains.

If this can all seem confusing, it is important to always remember that project management is a practical discipline. Theories, models and definitions are only useful in so far as they help to understand, apply and improve the practice of project management. As you get more and more involved in project management, the phrase will come to have a precise and helpful meaning to you in the specific environmental context you are working. This meaning will be developed through practice, rather than theory.

If you change the organisation you work for or type of projects you run, you will usually need to recalibrate the way you use the phrase project management relative to the new situation.

Project manager's checklist

■ Project management is a rich concept that covers a range of related elements and is associated closely with a wide set of components

■ The definition varies from sector to sector, and in some cases from function to function

■ Your definition should be calibrated to the context in which you work

---

case study

The value of understanding project management basics

Mary has been a project manager for over 15 years in the financial services sector. She is involved in IT projects, mostly introducing new systems and applications. Here she talks about the value of understanding project management basics.

'I have learned a lot since becoming a project manager about 15 years ago. For the first few years I was learning more and more advanced project management techniques, and getting used to applying them in practice. I still like to keep up to date and to expand my project management knowledge.

'But the funny thing is that as I get more experienced I have progressively realised the importance of understanding and applying the basics of project management. When I work with new project team members, project *sponsors* and *stakeholders* I often find myself having to explain some really basic project management concepts such as what a project is, what project management entails and so on. It's terribly important for everyone involved in the project to understand these things. If anyone does not they may struggle working on a project, or make decisions which are not in the project's interest.

'I have also learned that very few people are going to admit that they don't understand what projects are or why we use project management. So, the way I approach this is that at the start of every project I bring the team together, ideally including the sponsor and key stakeholders. The purpose of this meeting is to explain and ensure we share a common understanding of the project we are about to embark on. But in doing this I weave into my presentation fundamental project concepts. At worst I bore a few people, but generally I find this is very useful in helping the project to run smoothly.

'To do this, I have to give a very clear and meaningful explanation of basic project concepts. I think this is an important thing for all project managers to be able to do. It's surprising, but some experienced project managers struggle to do this.'

The role of the project manager

What is this about and why is it important?

Describing the role of a project manager seems straightforward once one understands the nature of projects and of *project management*. In reality, the project manager role is multi-faceted. It has different aspects which need to be stressed in different situations, depending on the nature of the project, the capabilities and behaviours of project team members, and the way the organisation supports or inhibits projects. It is important for project managers to understand these differences so they can apply the most appropriate aspects of the role in any situation.

Objectives

- To understand the different aspects of the role of project managers
- To explain why we need project managers

Common issues in achieving these objectives

- Inflexibility, applying a 'one size fits all' approach
- Limited experience of a wide variety of project situations

The guide

In this section I describe several of the most important aspects of the role of the project manager.

Aspect 1: execution of the project management process

The most obvious function of project managers is to execute the project management process and practices. Key elements of this role include:

■ scoping out the work to ensure there is a clear understanding why a project is being done, and what it will produce;

■ planning the project and determining what resources are required, how long it will take and how much it will cost;

■ getting the necessary resources allocated and ensuring every project team member knows what they are responsible for;

■ controlling the project and ensuring that it achieves its *objectives* within the planned time and cost;

■ completing the project properly to make sure everything produced by the project is of the quality expected and works as required;

■ ensuring problems or issues that may cause the completion of tasks to be delayed or stopped are resolved.

(In thinking this way, do not confuse means and ends. Project managers do not exist to execute project management. Project management is a toolkit for project managers to reliably, effectively and efficiently deliver projects. Consider an analogy: carpenters use wood-working tools, but they do not exist to use the tools. The tools exist to enable them to do their job.)

Aspect 2: dealing with human nature

Human nature is not always helpful to project delivery. A project manager has to deal with the reality of the behaviour of project team members.

One common reason for thinking we need project managers is the belief that people are lazy. If no-one chases them, they will not do their work. This is a weak justification for project management, but it would be naive to say that project managers never end up chasing people who otherwise would not do the work.

A more common trait is the so called 'student syndrome'. This is people's tendency to leave work until the deadline approaches. It will get done, but as late as possible. Generally, this is not helpful to efficient project delivery. Project managers regularly have to chase project team members to get the work done quickly.

Aspect 3: retaining focus

A more positive variant on the previous point is not that people are lazy or deliberately put things off, but that team members have too much to do. This is common, and is generally a failure of organisations to prioritise and load staff appropriately.

A common scenario is that team members are allocated part time to the project. The project work contends with everything else they need to do. Human nature is such that we tend to focus on the activities which we feel most pressured to do – the work of the person who shouts loudest or that with the closest deadline. In such circumstances, the project manager has to be one of the people shouting loudly! By chasing people, the work on the project gets prioritised above other activities they have to undertake, and the project progresses.

Chasing is a reality in many organisations, and a role that most project managers have to undertake. It is essential because of the failures to explicitly prioritise and load staff appropriately, but it is project management because of management failure. Better resource management helps to reduce this problem.

A related situation is when organisational processes and ways of working impede the execution of projects. A project manager is brought on to run a project 'outside' of normal operational processes. Good project managers can help project teams to overcome all sorts of obstacles. However, it is much better to find a long-term fix and improve the impeding processes – letting project managers focus on more value-adding tasks.

Aspect 4: providing expert help

Another reason for allocating a project manager to a project is because the project team does not have enough expertise in the project's subject matter: they need an expert guide. This can work – but it is a poor reason for using a project manager. Being the central expert in the subject matter is something different from being a project manager. My advice is that when you need an expert, hire an expert. If you need a project manager, hire a project manager.

My words have to be interpreted carefully here. I do not believe in generic project managers – the best project managers have experience in the subject matter and context of the project they are running. But this should be so they can apply project management in the most appropriate way and can enter into meaningful conversations with expert team members – not so they can play the expert.

For small projects an individual can act as both the project manager and the main expert, but these are different roles. As the projects get larger it becomes difficult for a single individual to combine both. My analogy is with the orchestra conductor. All conductors can play instruments, some brilliantly. But they do not conduct large orchestras whilst playing their instruments.

Aspect 5: dealing with risk and complexity

Sometimes project managers are employed to overcome failures in organisations or weaknesses in the project team. Many projects I have been involved in have required project managers for these reasons, but it is not the best use of skilled project managers' time.

A more positive justification for project management is that it is inherent within projects that there is a level of *risk* and a degree of complexity. There is a need for a dedicated role to manage this risk and this complexity.

Even perfect staff need alignment and co-ordination of their tasks. Someone needs to think about the logical ordering of tasks, and find the resources to do the work. Even perfect organisations face risks and need someone thinking about what the risks are and how they should be mitigated. No other role undertakes this managing of project complexity and risk.

Aspect 6: coaching and guiding the project team

A final role the project manager can take is as the guide and coach for the project team (see a related topic on p. 122). This role is similar to the one adopted by many *scrum masters* on *agile* projects.

Rather than planning and controlling, directing action and managing risks, a coach works with a project team to help them develop their own skills, build on strengths, overcome the problems they face and to approach projects with the right mindset. The attitude of a coach is that the project team is capable of delivering, but sometimes needs help in applying their own skills.

Acting as a coach can be a powerful and successful way of delivering a project if you have a mature team who are willing to take direct responsibility for delivering. It does not work in all situations. It generally needs a small team who are willing and able to self-organise, drive delivery and achieve the desired outcomes. One should not be quick to assume a team are not capable of this; many rise to the challenge if coached well. But there are risks, and project managers have to be confident and capable coaches before adopting this role.

It is best when project managers are flexible in the styles of management they adopt – sometimes monitoring, controlling and directing, at other times guiding, facilitating and coaching – depending on the needs of that situation.

Irrespective of the approach chosen, project managers should seek to manage the project team to be a high-performing team (see p. 55 for advice on high-performing project teams).

Project manager's checklist

- There are several aspects to the project manager's role
- Some aspects relate to the strength or weakness of the team, and overcoming organisational failures in resource allocation and prioritisation

- However, even in a perfect organisation with perfect teams there is a need to manage risk and co-ordinate the complexity of the tasks involved

- Depending on the nature of the team, the project and the environment, this risk and complexity management may be undertaken directly by the project manager – or by the project team with the project manager acting as a coach and guide

Customers, clients and users

What is this about and why is it important?

Project teams usually do not deliver for their own benefit. There are exceptions, such as in a business start-up. The team doing the start-up project are often simultaneously the owners, workers, users and *sponsors* of the project. This is an exceptional situation. More commonly, especially in large organisations and businesses, project teams are formed of specialised delivery staff who undertake the project for other individuals and groups.

In *project management* there is the concept of *stakeholders*, who are people or groups, mostly external to the project, who can impact or be impacted by a project. Such stakeholders need to be considered and managed by project teams. The concept of stakeholders is useful, but it is too simplistic to define everyone simply as a stakeholder. There are various stakeholders, with different needs and abilities to help or hinder the project. Project managers and project teams benefit from being clear about the types of stakeholders and the relationships required.

Not all stakeholders are of equal importance to the project. Sometimes their needs conflict and project teams have to find consensus or, more usually, determine whose needs should take precedence. There are often large numbers of stakeholders and project teams must determine whose interests to consider as stakeholders in the project.

This section looks at the categories of stakeholders typical projects have. (We discuss how to develop a productive relationship with them on p. 73.)

Objectives

- ▣ To show the different categories of stakeholders a project has

To help project teams in determining whose interests they will consider, and the relative priority between interests

Common issues in achieving these objectives

Simplistic views of stakeholder categories

Looking only at the needs close to a project and not wider enterprise needs

Imprecise use of terminology – such as lack of clarity using the word 'customer'

The guide

Different categories of stakeholder are identified by common roles and needs. Let us look at the most important ones:

1 **Project requirements owner:** the person or group of people who define the nature of the outputs from the project. These are the people who business analysts or deliverable designers should interview to develop requirement specifications.

2 **Enterprise requirements owner:** many projects not only have to conform to requirements to achieve the explicit end goals, but have further requirements for the wider benefit of the enterprise, or in some cases society as a whole. The direct customers of a project may not consider such requirements, but they are often critical. Included in this are applicable regulations, conformance to standards and operational requirements. Ensuring projects meet such requirements is an important part of project *governance*. This is an area that is often insufficiently considered, because of time or cost pressures, but can cause long-term problems if ignored.

3 **Pay master:** the person or group of people who finance the project. This is typically one or a few senior managers who are 'budget owners'.

4 **Resource provider:** the person or group of people who provides other resources, most typically people, to a project. For a project to gain such resources it is sometimes purely

a matter of having enough money to pay for the resources. But in most organisations resource providers have choices about where they allocate their team members. Then, part of the project manager's role in the early stages of a project is convincing such people to give them resources.

5 **Business case owner:** the person who has to justify the project and approve the project's business case. This is typically a senior manager.

6 **Benefits recipient:** the person or group of people who 'receive' the benefits at the end of the project. These are senior managers whose budgets or teams benefit from the successful delivery of the project.

7 **Sponsor:** the sponsor is normally a senior manager who acts as the bridge between the project and the rest of the organisation. This is a key role (which is described in detail on p. 66).

8 *Steering group*: the steering group is normally a small group of senior managers, chaired by the sponsor, who provides direction to the project and ensures it meets governance requirements. Usually part of the steering group's role is to make sure the project takes appropriate account of the interests of the wider stakeholder community.

9 **Deliverables users or end-users:** the people who have to live with the final deliverables. For example, in an IT project these are the users of applications; in a construction project these are the people who live in, work in or otherwise use the building.

10 **The project team:** the project team do not just work on a project, they have an interest in it. This may be with regard to personal development, performance ratings, enjoyment in the project work or work-life balance.

11 **Other affected parties:** there may be a large range of other people who are impacted by projects in different ways. This is often the most hazy group to identify and manage. There is both a risk that projects insufficiently consider their needs or become over focused on trying to manage the needs of

too many stakeholders of this type. Such stakeholders may be internal or external to an organisation and can include suppliers, customers, regulators and employees.

The stakeholder balance

The answer to the question 'Which stakeholders should be considered?' is specific to an individual project working in a certain context. There may be one person who fulfils all stakeholder roles, but that is unusual. A more typical situation is when there are many stakeholders, but some of them have many 'hats', i.e. they fit into multiple categories.

The key for a project is to find the right balance, ensuring:

- All critical interests are reflected in the project's work.
- The set of stakeholders is broad enough, but no broader. Too few stakeholders may mean important needs are missed out. Too many stakeholders create inefficiencies – sometimes huge inefficiencies.
- There is alignment between the interests of different stakeholders.

Let us briefly focus on this last point, as it is a source of many problems and risks on projects. There are some obvious areas where alignment between the different stakeholders is required. It is helpful if some of the stakeholder roles are performed by the same people. For example, in conjunction with the above list:

- Stakeholders 3, 5 and 6: aligning paying for a project, with authorising it and achieving the benefits. Additionally, it is usually beneficial to align this with role 7. Good sponsorship often comes from those who have most to gain from a project. I think of these aligned needs as the client interests in the project – but some would call this the customer interests.
- Stakeholders 1 and 9: have the primary people who define the requirements that deliverables should fulfil, as they are the people who will use them. I think of these aligned needs

as the end-user interests of a project, but confusingly, some people also call this the customer interests. Lack of clarity of who is being pointed to when project teams, sponsors and steering groups talk about customers is a common source of issues.

In most situations, there are multiple stakeholders. Unless their interests are aligned the project may get into trouble. Examples of this include:

▪ Misalignment between stakeholder 3 and stakeholders 1, 2 and 6: in this situation the person paying for a project may not be willing to pay for all the requirements needed, or not be concerned whether the project will enable the person who has to deliver the benefits to actually deliver them.

▪ Misalignment between stakeholder 8 and stakeholder 11: in this case a *steering committee* may direct a project to take insufficient account of the needs of the people impacted by a project.

In both of these examples it is possible that this misalignment is deliberate. A pay master may sensibly wish to restrain the excessive desires of requirements owners. Steering committees may need to push projects through in spite of the impact on other stakeholders. But such choices should be deliberate and based on an understanding of the implications, taking account of the effect on the project and its outcome. A project may seem to be progressing fine without considering all the stakeholder needs, but sooner or later problems will arise if they are not adequately considered.

Project manager's checklist

▪ There are multiple categories of stakeholders on projects

▪ Project teams should assess the relevant stakeholders for their project in their specific situation

▪ Significant problems and risks arise on projects when key stakeholder groups are ignored, or their interests are misaligned

two

Setting up your project

When project management is discussed in an abstract way, it can be a dry topic. What makes project management interesting is using it to deliver real projects.

This part explains how to turn an abstract idea into a real project. First it explores how to define your project. Projects are specific endeavours leading to specific outcomes. To achieve this, a clear definition of a particular project is essential. The next section looks at the subjects of deliverables and benefits realisation. The third section discusses the resources needed to deliver a project. The final section brings these thoughts together in the topic of project planning. The project plan is one of the central tools of project management.

This part's content underpins most of the other parts of this text.

Defining your project

What is this about and why is it important?

Projects exist to deliver a defined outcome, in an agreed time and within cost. As a project progresses the outcome may be modified, as may the constraints under which it is delivered. But such changes need to be done in a controlled and agreed manner, against a clearly understood, accepted and documented baseline.

Different styles of *project management* place varying emphasis on the level of detail and time horizon in objectives, use differing names for objectives and scope, and have a range of approaches to changing them. But all forms of project management have some concept of objectives and scope.

Various commentators on project management use different terminology – and can argue strongly about the differences, for example, between goals, objectives and outcomes. In a short section like this I do not want to get into this debate, as it loses sight of the most important point: projects need a stable set of words which give a sense of direction and can answer the question 'Why are we doing this project?': I call this *objectives*. The second question is 'How far should we go to achieve those objectives?': the answer to this question I call *scope*. It is the combination of scope and objectives which is the basis for shaping, designing, planning and managing the project.

Clarifying objectives and scope is a key early activity in the delivery of every successful project.

Objectives

- To explain the importance of objectives and scope
- To understand how to define the objectives and scope of a project

Common issues in achieving these objectives

→ Tendency to worry about the 'what' and 'how' of a project rather than the 'why'

→ Poor analysis and questioning skills in extracting this information from project *stakeholders*

→ Careless project management accepting poor definitions

→ Highly volatile situations in which objectives and scope are inherently ambiguous or unstable

The guide

Three factors go towards defining a project:

1 **Objectives:** *why* are you doing the project? When you have finished it what will have been achieved?

2 **Scope:** how broad or narrow are the boundaries of the project to achieve your objectives?

3 **How clear and stable the objectives and scope are:** can they be made unambiguous and stable, or are they inherently vague and continuously changing? This impacts how you design and manage your project, and even the style of project management.

In this section I deal with defining scope and objectives, but not handling instability, vagueness or change in them. This is a complex topic, and is touched on later (see pp. 94, 142 and 190). There is a further level of detailed definitions beyond objectives, normally called requirements which are contained in the requirements specification, which are outside the scope of this book.

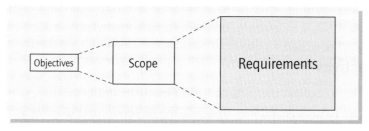

Objectives, scope and requirements

Whilst the project manager should ensure that objectives and scope are clear, they or the project team do not create scope or objectives. They are defined by the project stakeholders. However, stakeholders usually struggle to do this without help from the project team. Practical issues with stakeholders defining what they want are discussed later (see p. 217).

Objectives

It is essential to have a clear understanding of a project's objectives, as this sets the direction for the whole endeavour. Objectives should answer the question *why* the project is being done, but not *what* or *how* it will be done. A project should have at least one objective, written in the form of short statements, and sometimes only one sentence long.

Objectives are best defined with input from stakeholders and the project *sponsor*. A good approach is to:

- Start by thinking through why the project is being done. What it will achieve? This should not be a broad intention, but a specific, unambiguous and clear goal.
- Ask the question: if this objective is met would the organisation be different from how it is today?
- Check – if there are multiple objectives are they consistent and compatible? A project to increase staff satisfaction is not usually compatible with one to reduce headcount, whereas a project to improve customer satisfaction is compatible with one to improve product quality.
- Write the objectives down. If you cannot write them down they are not yet useful or usable objectives.
- You should be able to write each objective in one or two sentences. An objective which takes several lines to write down is usually not one but multiple objectives. If your objective is long or has phrases linked by 'and' then separate it into its component parts.
- Make sure that the objectives are of sufficient quality. Get the wording right. A quality objective is: correct, clear, meaningful, unambiguous and concise.

- Do a commonsense check: are these objectives something worthwhile for the organisation to achieve?
- Review and confirm the objectives with the project sponsor and key stakeholders.
- Produce a final documented version of the objectives and subject it to *change control*.

(Adapted from *Brilliant Checklists for Project Managers*, by Richard Newton, Pearson Education, 2012)

Scope

It is essential to have a clear understanding of a project's scope as this sets the boundaries for the whole endeavour. A project scope should be formally documented. Typically, the scope can be written in anything from a few lines to several pages depending on the scale and complexity of the project. The scope is not a definition of the project, but a definition of the limits to the project.

Scope is also best defined with input from stakeholders and the project sponsor, ideally when the objectives are clear. The best approach when defining scope is to ask questions in the style of the following:

- What are the overall boundaries of the project?
    - Can you write down what is 'in' and 'out'?
    - Are you dependent on anything that is outside the project's scope?
- What are the deliverables?
    - Are you working to deliver a set of tangible deliverables or provide a service or capability?
    - Are you working to deliver independent deliverables or an integrated end-to-end solution?
    - How will the quality of deliverables be determined?
    - Are there any deliverables required by the project which it is not responsible for?

▩ Are you working to implement a specific solution, or to solve a problem?

  – Are you responsible for producing deliverables or achieving business benefits?

▩ How is the customer going to measure success at the end of the project?

▩ What can be modified from the customers' viewpoint?

  – Is predictability more important, or speed to deliver?

  – Is cost or time more important?

  – How much *risk* can you take to achieve the project objectives?

▩ Are there any other constraints on the project?

  – Are there any external considerations?

  – What are the time or budget constraints?

▩ How do your customers want to work with you?

  – How will decisions be made on the project?

  – How high is the project in your customers' priorities?

  – Can your sponsor allocate the required resources or do other stakeholders need to be involved?

  – Who can legitimately place requirements upon the project?

▩ Are there any other customer *assumptions* or needs that are not explicit?

(Adapted from *The Project Manager: Mastering the Art of Delivery*, by Richard Newton, Pearson Education, 2010)

Having defined the scope there should then be a check. Ask yourself: can you achieve the objectives within the scope defined, or does it need to be altered to achieve the objectives?

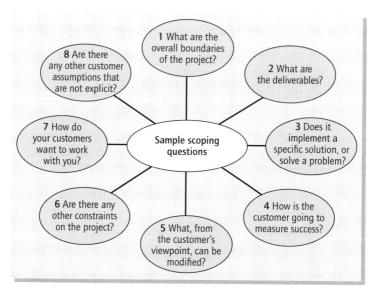

Sample scoping questions

Project manager's checklist

- Defined, clear objectives and scope are essential for a well-run project

- Objectives describe why a project is being undertaken, and provide a sense of direction to the project team

- Scope describes the boundaries or limits of the project

case study

Clarity of scope

Paul works for an insurance company in a central project management office (PMO) *function. He joined the PMO after working as a project manager for a number of years. As a PMO member he is involved in* the quality assurance (QA) *of projects. He shares some of his lessons from performing QAs.*

'I'm regularly involved in project reviews. The way I do a review is to work with a project manager over a period of time. The purpose of the review is not to tell people off, or to assess their performance, but to identify areas of risk related to the way projects are run, and by doing this to help project teams to be successful.

'I can list a whole lot of different reasons why projects go wrong. Many of the project managers I know are good at what they do. They know how to produce a plan, how to manage the plan, how to assess and manage risks, how to keep their teams engaged. These are not always easy tasks, so I have to applaud their skills. But everyone can improve with the right help.

'If I think about all the projects I have ever reviewed a pattern emerges. This pattern shows the most common mistakes project managers make. In reality, even though I think of most of the project managers I work with as pretty experienced they tend to make some basic mistakes.

'The most common mistake is not to be crystal clear on the project's objectives and to have an ambiguous project scope. If you don't get these things clear – no matter how good the rest of your project management is – the project will be problematic!'

Objectives, deliverables and tasks

What is this about and why is it important?

In the previous section we looked at project definition: understanding *objectives* and *scope*. Although critical information, this is not the right sort of information to develop a project plan from. Before you can plan, objectives must be converted. Objectives define *why* you want to do a project. There are two processes that convert this *why* into something a project team can plan with: translation and decomposition.

Translation converts the *why* into *what*, *how*, *who* and *when*: *what* is needed to achieve the *why*, *how* can this be developed, *who* will do the development, and *when* they will do it. The process of planning (described on p. 39), deals with the *who* and the *when*. This section focuses on the first parts of translation: determining the *what* and the *how*.

The second process is called *decomposition*. A set of objectives can be translated into a 'big' what and a 'big' how. In decomposition the *what* and the *how* are broken down into smaller and smaller constituents until they are small enough to understand, plan and control. For example, if the objective is to stay safe, dry and warm, this can be fulfilled by having a house, and that can be achieved by building it. A what of 'a house' and a how of 'build it' are decomposed into a detailed description of the design of the house and all the steps needed to build it. The project can then be planned.

The combination of translation and decomposition converts an understanding of objectives into clearly actionable tasks that can be allocated to named individuals, estimated and controlled. Accurate and suitable translation and decomposition are essential for good planning and successful project delivery.

Objectives

- To convert project objectives into clearly actionable tasks
- To develop the optimal structure for planning and managing a project

Common issues in achieving these objectives

→ Inaccurate translation

→ Mixing and confusing the decomposition of the what and the how

→ Decomposition to wrong and inconsistent levels of detail

→ Over-hasty translation and decomposition without sufficient critical review

The guide

Terminology

Different styles of planning use different terminologies, but the underlying activities of translation and decomposition and the challenges that go with them remain the same.

I am going to stick with the classic language of *project management*. The *why* is called objectives, the *what* is deliverables, and the *how* is the tasks that will go into the project plan. (I use the terms task and activity interchangeably.) So objectives are translated into deliverables, and deliverables into tasks. The deliverables and tasks are then decomposed into details.

Alternative terminologies exist. For example, the *why* may be defined as business needs, the *what* as a set of business capabilities that fulfil that need, and the *how* as the actions to develop the capabilities. More complex translation schemas are possible. I describe a three-layer translation from objective to deliverable to tasks, but you may come across more layers.

Translation

Like real translation, no reliable algorithm exists for converting objectives into deliverables and deliverables into the tasks. This is a process of analysis, creative thinking, application of experience and subject matter expertise. It also requires a willingness to reflect and challenge the translations being made: are they accurate and complete?

A good practical approach to do this is to brainstorm with the project team. Sticky notes are a great way of doing this – thinking, writing them down, sticking them on a wall, and then arranging them into a hierarchy. The aim is to have a complete translation to a common level of granularity. (Chapter 3 of my book *Project Management Step by Step* (Pearson Education, 2006) has a description of this quick and easy process.)

Decomposition

Decomposition is intellectually simpler than translation, but can be tricky to get right. I regularly see plans that have decomposed large tasks into incomplete and inconsistent sets of smaller activities. The aim of decomposition is to get to elements of a scale that can be planned.

For planning, deliverable decomposition is required to reach the level at which deliverables are sufficiently understood to be translated into tasks. Sometimes this is a fairly high level of detail, on other occasions lower-level detail is required. (Note that further deliverable decomposition is also often required for design and development activities. Where detailed definition is required for design and development, this is not used in planning, but is described in requirements specifications.)

From a planning perspective, the right level of decomposition is achieved when the tasks can be allocated to individuals in the project team, can be estimated, and when they are sufficiently small that they can be managed when they are performed. Typically, I like tasks that can be allocated in 1–4 week chunks. Some project approaches, such as *agile* insist on a more granular decomposition which enables daily reviews of progress.

One goal of task decomposition is to split tasks into a similar level of detail. This is typically greater for the tasks you will be undertaking soon, and then the level of decomposition is progressively less the further into the future the tasks will be performed. This approach is known as *progressive elaboration.*

A common name in project management for the resultant decomposition hierarchy is a *work breakdown structure (WBS).*

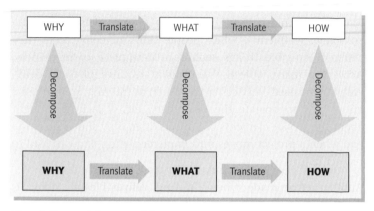

Translation and decomposition

Practical approaches and challenges

Each element of objectives, deliverable and tasks can be decomposed, but they form different hierarchies and should not be confused. If you develop a hierarchy that mixes objective, deliverable and task decomposition it will soon become unintelligible and unmanageable. In the end, you manage tasks – checking that they are progressing towards deliverables. You then test deliverables – checking they fulfil the objectives.

Performing translation and decomposition requires expertise in the subject matter of the project. If a project is to build a house, you need to understand how a house breaks down into its constituents parts. This must be done by relevant experts, not just by a project manager alone (unless the project manager happens to be an expert in the project domain).

There is not only one possible translation of objectives, and not all translations are equally good. In this case, 'good' means providing an effective and efficient way to understand, communicate, monitor and control the project. The process of translation drives the way the project and the project team are managed. When you translate and decompose a set of objectives and you are not happy with the resultant plan, try a different translation and decomposition.

Make sure translations of objectives into deliverables are complete. Frequently, when people think of deliverables they think of tangible things such as a new piece of machinery. Achieving many objectives not only requires physical deliverables, but needs services as well, such as training, so new users know how to operate the machinery, etc. A lack of thought about the service elements of projects often only shows up at the end when a project moves into implementation and can lead to project failure.

Another error made when defining deliverables in detail is thinking in terms of how a deliverable will be used, but not how it will perform or be operated. For instance, the world of IT splits deliverable definition into two sets of requirements: functional (covering the actual functions of the software) and non-functional (covering aspects such as performance and operating conditions). It is always worth asking about the operational characteristics of any deliverable. For example, if you are building a house you not only need to know how big it will be and what fixtures and fittings it requires (functional requirements), but also how long it is built to last, what weather conditions it should withstand and what building requirements it has to conform to (non-functional requirements).

I have described translation and decomposition as if they are sequential activities. In reality, they are done at the same time. The brain bounces between translation and decomposition as the two processes feed off each other. Once you feel you have completed translation and decomposition you need to check the output. Critical review is essential and the following ideas will help in this review:

- Apply a concept from the consultancy group McKinsey: 'MECE'. This is an acronym for *mutually exclusive, cumulatively exhaustive.* The results from the translation and decomposition of objectives must be MECE. If they are not mutually exclusive, then you risk duplicating work. If they are not cumulatively exhaustive, you risk missing elements and so fail to achieve your objectives.

▪ Check the level of granularity in your decomposition. Is it consistent, and sufficient but not excessive?

▪ Finally, check back against the original scope. Are the deliverables and tasks proposed within the original scope? An efficient and effective plan has everything required to achieve the objectives, within the defined scope and only that.

Project manager's checklist

▪ To develop a project plan, the objectives (why) should be translated into deliverables (what) and then tasks (how)

▪ The deliverables and tasks should be decomposed into sufficient detail to enable understanding, communication, control and management

Building a plan

What is this about and why is it important?

Planning is the foundation on which *project management* builds. Arguably it is project planning that differentiates project management from other styles of management more than anything else. Huge amounts have been written about planning. There are many opinions about how to plan and many complexities involved, for example: how to reliably decompose a large task into smaller ones; how to estimate time, resources and costs; and how to deal with unknowns and volatility. However, the fundamental principles of planning are relatively simple.

There are different styles, duration and approaches to planning. This section provides a generic overview and points to other sections to provide a deeper understanding.

Objectives

- To explain why projects need plans
- To provide an understanding of how to plan
- To indicate areas for further study

Common issues in achieving these objectives

- Insufficient effort
- Planning treated as an end in itself, not a means
- Lack of consideration of how the plan will be used
- Counter-productive management behaviour and organisational culture

The guide

Which plan?

The first challenge is to define what we mean by 'the plan'. When you ask to see a project's plan, different artefacts may be presented: perhaps an enormous Gantt chart on a wall, maybe an *agile backlog* in *Jira*, or possibly a lengthy word document. This reflects different styles of planning, and also differing views on what the plan entails. There are work schedules, resource plans, *quality plans*, *risk* plans, communications plans and so on. You can get into word games as well – between the 'project plan' and the 'project management plan'. The Project Management Institute (*PMI*) defines a project management plan as an object which 'defines how the project is executed, monitored and controlled, and closed'. This is a much broader concept than that dealt with in this book.

In this section, I focus on the plan in a traditional sense: a set of structured information that defines the what, when and who: what needs to be done, when it will be done, who will do it. This can be presented in different formats. You should get this information right irrespective of presentation format.

The uses of project plans

Unless you know what a plan will be used for, and by whom, then you risk developing or presenting the wrong sort of plan. In general, plans fulfil the following functions. They:

- provide an understanding of the activities and risks in a project;
- show how long a project will take, what resources will be required and how much it will cost to do;
- help communicate and explain the project to project *stakeholders* and project team members;
- facilitate the allocation of work to project team members;
- enable monitoring and controlling projects towards successful completions;
- enable co-ordinating dependencies between projects;
- support expectation management, business planning, management decision and commitment making.

Before starting to develop a project plan it is important to understand that plans have multiple uses and users.

How to plan

The first step in planning is to decide the overall approach you will take to the project. The plan is a reflection of how you want to develop and manage the project. If you do not understand this, you cannot plan effectively.

Next decide on the most appropriate time horizon to plan over. This is not necessarily the life of the project. If a project lasts for years, you generally cannot predict reliably years into the future. Hence the concept of *progressive elaboration*, where you plan in progressively more detail the closer the activities in the plan are to the present.

Once you have decided on these factors, the steps in planning are conceptually straightforward:

- **Decompose:** convert the project deliverables into tasks. Then break the tasks into smaller tasks until the tasks can be allocated to individual owners and the time they will take estimated (see p. 33).
- **Structure:** arrange the activities into a meaningful hierarchy. Ideally, this hierarchy enables key milestones to be identified.
- **Identify dependencies:** link tasks by the appropriate dependencies.
- **Identify resources required:** identify the resource types and quantities to fulfil the plan.
- **Determine timescales:** work out how long each task will take with the resources required.
- **Align to resources available:** align what you theoretically need with what is actually available.
- **Add contingency:** contingency is a reflection of the degree of risk in a plan (and should not be a reflection of the planner's skill level!).
- **Iterate the plan:** work to align the activities in the plan with the resources available and the timescale required. This is usually about making compromises. Planning will not make the impossible possible, all it does is make the reality of the situation clear.

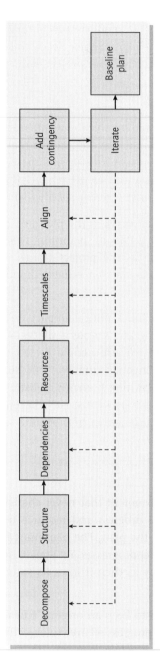

Planning steps

The next step is to get the plan approved by the project *sponsor* and key stakeholders. This normally results in further debate and compromises to align the plan to their needs and priorities. But once this is achieved you have your project plan.

Who to involve in planning

The project manager should involve the whole team in planning. It is the team's plan as much as the project manager's. Teams who develop plans, rather than have them imposed on them, are more likely to go the extra mile to deliver the resulting project. There are techniques such as *planning poker* which help in this.

Ideally, involve key stakeholders in the planning process. Invite them to be full participants in planning workshops. Then it is their plan as much as the project team's. This will ease future conversations with and encourage support from such stakeholders.

Management behaviour has a critical impact on planning. Do managers regard planning as a serious activity, or as something that lip service is paid to? Are people forced to commit to estimates without contingency and without sufficient information? Are expected planning horizons realistic or not? There are no easy answers to such problems, but you must be aware of them so you can try to take action to moderate such behaviour (see p. 136).

Maintaining project plans

A plan is not a static document that never changes. As soon as the project starts actual progress and resource usage will vary from what is defined in the plan. The plan must be maintained and updated as the project progresses. Yet you do not want a plan that is altering every day as then it loses its value as a tool for prediction and control.

The normal approach is to keep an original *baseline plan* which is used to report formal progress relative to objectives. A separate plan is maintained to see where you actually are and to make accurate forward-looking predictions. There is a tendency for the variance between the actual and baseline plan to grow over time. On a periodic basis, with the approval of the sponsor and stakeholders the baseline plan is updated to bring it in line with the actual plan.

Challenges in planning

The process of planning is simple to understand, but hard to execute effectively. It not only requires skills and knowledge but also judgement. A plan is never perfect, but can be good enough. Deciding what is good enough is a challenge for novice project managers who sometimes plan in too little detail, but more often try to plan in too much detail over a longer time horizon than is practical or value adding. A plan is a tool, and when the tool is good enough use it.

Other problems in planning include:

- not being clear about *objectives* and *scope* (see p. 26);
- not being clear about how to achieve these objectives within this scope (see p. 33);
- estimating and resourcing (see p. 46);
- risk (see pp. 94 and 108);
- management behaviour and attitudes to planning (see pp. 136 and 142);
- setting the wrong time horizon for planning – trying to plan accurately beyond the horizon of predictability (see p. 142);
- excessive and unnecessary multi-tasking (see pp. 113 and 172).

Final planning thoughts

A plan is most useful when it enables the team to manage their time completely. If your project approach has logs for items such as issues and risks, that is fine. But to really resolve issues, risks, impediments and so on, they all need to be worked on. They may be logged and tracked independently (using issues logs, risk logs, etc.), but the work takes time and needs to be factored into people's workloads, or else you cannot prioritise time properly. Time for these activities also needs to be factored into the plan. This may be by not loading staff 100% and leaving time for other work, through contingency, or by explicitly including resolution as planned tasks. Whichever approach is chosen, planning at 100% utilisation and assuming no issues, risks or impediments will occur is naive and *will* result in you running late.

Planning is a means and is not an end in itself. If it is not driving action then you are doing it incorrectly or wasting your time. Plans predict into the future. But as a tool the important thing is what you do next. Plan so you can predict, but also plan so you know what you must do *today*.

Finally, reward the team for progress against the plan. But do not lose sight of the fact that it is not how much you have done that is most important, but how far you have to go.

Project manager's checklist

■ Planning is one of the central parts of project management. Without a plan, there is no project

■ To develop a good plan you must be clear about what it is for and how it will be used

■ A plan is a tool for project management – it is not an end in itself. It needs to be good enough, not perfect

■ Planning is conceptually simple, but can be hard in practice

Estimating and resourcing

What is this about and why is it important?

Estimating is the process of determining how much time and resources a project requires. Resourcing is the subsequent process of identifying and allocating the right resources to a project. Estimating and resourcing regularly cause headaches for project managers. The practices often vary significantly from the theory and are the topics of many debates.

Being able to estimate the resources required to run a project and gaining access to those resources are central to managing projects. Without estimating, a plan is just a task list. When estimates are included it becomes a powerful tool for making commitments, prediction, measurement and control. What then makes the plan real is applying resources to the tasks in the plan.

There are many challenges involved in estimating and resourcing. This section provides some important tips to overcome these challenges. Estimating is possibly the most difficult part of *project management,* and the ability to estimate accurately is a sign of a subject matter expert.

Objectives

- To give an idea of how to estimate and resource a project
- To overview common challenges in estimating and resourcing
- To provide some tips for avoiding these problems

Common issues in achieving these objectives

- Estimating independently of the reality of available resources
- Estimations made without involvement of sufficient parties
- Lack of resources available to a project

The guide

What to plan and estimate

Estimation is the activity that links the resources required on a project with the activities required to complete the project. In estimating, project managers determine the time a project will take, and what it will cost.

Any of the resources required to do the activities in the plan may need to be estimated. This most obviously includes people to do the work (human resources) and money. There are different categories of people and money that have to be managed in different ways. On top of this, there may be items that need to be bought, hired or borrowed to carry out the project, and facilities which need to be booked. If these resources are free and easily available, they can be ignored for planning purposes. But anything in short supply or subject to other constraints, such as long lead times, must be planned.

In this section I am going to mention people and money, but the principles apply to all resources.

The theory and the reality

The theory of planning is conceptually simple. Identify what needs to be done (the tasks or activities), and then estimate the resources required to undertake these activities in the timescale available.

The first difficulty is simply that estimating is complex. Another is that resources are not homogeneous. You do not just want any resource, you want the right resources. The specific resources the project is allocated impacts the estimates. For example, you do not need just anyone on the project team – you need people with the right skills, availability and style to work productively in the team.

Estimation is difficult and brings all sorts of real-world considerations to light. Projects are unique, and therefore cannot be simply estimated by direct reference to an exactly equivalent prior project. On the other hand, most projects are similar to some degree to previous projects, and even if the whole project is not, individual tasks often are, so having previous experience helps.

Most projects operate within some constraints which limit the freedom to develop the ideal project plan. Such constraints may include the need to complete a project by a fixed date, limited money, time windows when money can and cannot be spent, or people without all the desired skills. The available team members may be geographically dispersed, which does not facilitate easy working (see p. 60). Often people are only available part time which increases elapsed times to get tasks completed as well as the logistical complexity.

There is almost always a difference between the resources you get and what your plan might require. This means plans must be developed iteratively, cycling between resourcing and estimating several times. Resourcing and estimating can be thought of as different facets of one planning process. Also, even when the project is planned and running, resource management is an ongoing part of project work. It is not uncommon for project managers to complain that they should be managing the project and are not resource managers. Rightly or wrongly, resource management is central to many project managers' work.

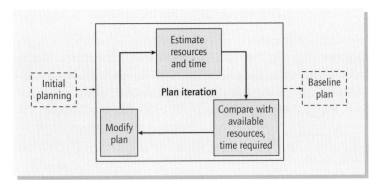

Plan iteration

Another issue project managers have to deal with is that agreements concerning resources made at the start of a project are not always kept for the life of the project. Sometimes this is because of perceived failings in the projects, changes in *stakeholders*, or changes in the business environment. Most typically this results in budget cuts or headcount freezes. In some situations these can be predicted and planned for – in others they just have to be responded to when they occur.

Tips for resourcing

An issue for project staffing comes down to the fact that most businesses are not organised for projects, but are arranged in functional groups or around operational processes. This may be sensible, but it does not help projects.

Consider the tendency of businesses to set up shared resource pools which projects must use for certain key tasks. This often leads to project inefficiencies. Shared resource pools go under many names: centres of excellence, offshore teams, expert groups and so on. Whatever the name shared resource pools often mistake resource efficiency (having everyone 100% busy) with project efficiency (the best way to deliver the project). They are not the same thing and can be competing *objectives*.

If you are a project manager, aim for the best way to deliver the project. If some of your resources come from shared resource pools try to get individuals allocated to the project for 100% of the time you need them, even if this means they are sometimes less than 100% busy. If they time slice between your project and others the inefficiency will grow and the duration of the project will increase significantly.

However, it would be naive to assume that all resources can be allocated 100% to a project. Not everyone has the luxury of working on one thing at a time. But whenever people are multi-tasking between the project and other activities, the project manager should at least try to challenge the situation, and make sure decision makers understand the implications of multi-tasking on efficiency (see p. 113).

Where resources are constrained or impaired in some way the answer is not always to seek additional resources. Limited resources can be at least partially handled by picking the best people, and managing the project team for high performance (see p. 55).

Tips for estimating

Like anything else on the project, the project manager must see that estimating is done, but they do not have to personally undertake it. No-one can estimate something they know nothing about. If you know nothing about something then you are not estimating, you are guessing!

Estimation is best done by the most expert people in the team, with the greatest familiarity with the task in hand. However, even without full expertise, we can normally find something that is more or less similar to what is currently being proposed and use this as a model to guide estimation. Additionally, the *decomposition* of project tasks ideally breaks activities into chunks of work that can be estimated. However, this is a partial help at best. Estimating 10 small unknown tasks is not inherently any easier than estimating one big unknown task! Decomposition in an unknown situation may simply result in a false sense of accurate structured thinking.

Estimating works best as a group activity, taking inputs and views from different team members. Whoever is consulted, do not divorce making estimates from the people doing the work. Estimates are not only useful as a planning guide, but also as a basis for commitment making. People are more likely to commit to estimates they themselves have made than those imposed by someone else.

If you know there will be a fixed and constrained pool of resources, start by estimating the times the available resources will take to do the project, rather than planning around perfect resourcing levels. The problem of lack of or limited resources should be factored into plans at the outset and not treated as a surprise!

As a result of the uncertainty, ambiguity and *risk* inherent in every project, it is good practice to add contingency to project plans. Contingency is essential in many projects. The future is not completely predictable and even the best plans will contain errors and have a level of risk associated with them. Regrettably, contingency may be perceived as 'fat' in the plan. It is unfortunate when line management regard contingency as fat – but this is reinforced by project teams treating contingency as something it is their automatic right to use.

It is generally better to keep a single 'pot' of contingency centrally, or at least as few 'pots' as possible. This way it can be managed and allocated when required. If contingency is just included as a common overhead in every task it will be taken as the baseline and automatically used up. When this happens the project ends up taking more time than necessary.

Project managers tend to focus on the risk of underestimation. They want to ensure the project does not run out of time or money. Their line managers are often more concerned with overestimation, and see their role as squeezing fat out of projects. In reality, each should be concerned with both!

To avoid this, project managers and their line managers should explicitly agree what is important. In some organisational cultures it is unacceptable to be late or to overspend – and in these circumstances it is better, or at least prudent, to overestimate. Generally, projects should try to be as efficient and effective as possible, giving accurate predictions to an acceptable level of risk, but only over-running when these prove to be wrong. On an aggregate level, it is better for organisations to encourage accurate planning and accept some projects will over-run, than penalise over-running and have all projects build in sufficient leeway to avoid this.

Project managers and teams will naturally be judged by their performance, but this needs to be done with care. Planning and estimating should be the basis for controlling the project and not directly for performance management. Linking performance assessments directly to a project team's history of delivery to time and budget simply results in rampant over-estimations and elongated plans.

Project manager's checklist

- Resourcing and estimating are interlinked facets of the planning process

- The theory of estimating often differs dramatically from the practice

- Resource management is an ongoing task for the life of the project

- Estimating should draw on the skills of the whole team – and be used for creating commitment as well as determining timescales and costs

- Line management behaviour and performance management affect project estimates

three

Utilising the team, sponsor and stakeholders

When we think of projects we often think of future visions, complicated plans and great endeavours. But the heart of a project is not the vision, the plan or the deliverables: it is the project team.

It is the project team that the project manager manages, and which does the work on the project. Overseeing this team is the project sponsor. Beyond the project team and sponsor are a range of other stakeholders who may be interested in or impacted by the project, or the project may need some support from. In other words, project management is people management.

Traditional project management techniques did not focus enough on the human side of project management. Fortunately, over the past decades, the human factors in project management have been given more prominence. This part looks at the human factors: what is a good project team and how do you create one; how do you deal with the challenges of multi-location and even multi-national project teams; what are the secrets to having a good project sponsor; and what is the best way of engaging and managing stakeholders?

The high-performance project team

What is this about and why is it important?

It is the project team that creates deliverables and achieves outcomes, not the project manager. As in an orchestra the project manager may be the essential conductor, but the players make the music. The project manager's work (planning, managing issues and *risks*, encouraging sponsors and so on) is forgotten once the project completes. What is left and is of value are the outputs from the project team – the deliverables.

There are huge variations in the effectiveness of different teams. High-performance teams deliver substantially more than poorly performing or even average teams, sometimes several times as much. Experiencing truly high-performance teams is exciting, fun and provides real learning.

The project manager's role is critical in creating a high-performance team. Unless you are lucky, such good project teams do not just happen. They are selected, created and sustained – mostly by project managers, ideally with the assistance of *sponsors* and *stakeholders*. Unfortunately, this aspect of the project manager's role is often overlooked.

Objectives

- To understand what makes a high-performing team
- To help project managers and sponsors develop productive project teams

Common issues in achieving these objectives

- Excessive focus on technical aspects of *project management* whilst overlooking the human aspects
- Lack of awareness of high-performance teams' characteristics
- General lack of skills in team development amongst project managers

The guide

Building a productive project team has specific challenges. Project teams are typically short-term structures yet forming productive teams takes time. Many project managers, even good ones, focus on the technical aspects of project management (e.g. planning, issue and *risk management*) above the human aspects. Project management training tends not to focus on people management and motivation. Some project managers and teams have never been part of a high-performance team, and so they do not know what to aim for or how much is possible. Yet without aiming high, you are unlikely to achieve the best result.

All of these are resolvable issues, and given enough emphasis, project managers can build productive teams with increased creativity and output.

High-performance project teams

The most productive teams have a certain culture. They are action, outcome and team orientated, so let us have a closer look at such teams.

First of all, individuals in high-performance teams feel part of the project – helping the project manager to identify and resolve issues and risks, as well as doing their explicitly allocated work. Team members put the goals of the team above their individual goals. Individuals have specific responsibilities which they strive to achieve, but everyone delivers together. When someone has a problem, it is not just an individual's problem – others contribute to identify and implement solutions. Everyone feels that success or failure is shared.

It is not always true, but such teams are usually fun. If everyone is miserable then the chances are you are not working in a high-performance team. (Although being fun does not, alone, mean it is a high-performance team!)

High-performance teams tend to be more creative, finding better approaches and ways around issues and risks. However, what really differentiates the most highly performing teams is the speed with which they progress – both in terms of the project work and in resolving impediments to progress. From the highest performance team you will not hear that someone is waiting for a reply to an email, or nothing can be done until a meeting occurs in a month's time. They find their way around such progress barriers.

How do you develop such a team?

Developing such a team starts with the choice of people in the team. Obviously, you must have the capabilities and skills to do the work required, or the resources and time to learn how. However, attitude is usually more important than absolute skills excellence. It is a cliché – but true – you need team players, not star individuals or lone heroes.

When it comes to the people in the team always go for quality over quantity: do not think in terms of 'my plan shows me I need 10 people', think in terms of 'what are the best people I can get within the project budget?'

Once you have a team give its members clarity. Every team member should understand the desired outcome, and be absolutely clear about their role and responsibilities. Most important is clarity about the expected behaviour and how the project will work. *RACI charts* and responsibility definitions are powerful tools you should use, but they are never foolproof. You want team members who are empowered to resolve issues and gaps in responsibilities.

Providing such clarity is not a quick exercise. It is one of the project manager's most important activities and time should be invested to make sure it is done correctly.

Team members will be motivated if they feel they will benefit from the project. Occasionally, this may be as simple as a personal belief in the project goals. Consider also what you can give back to every team member. This does not need to be major or difficult: perhaps some training, learning on the job, exposure to senior managers or new ways of working. Often, if the team is highly performing, the satisfaction and fun of being part of it is sufficient.

Push the team hard, expect high output and set the example yourself. Allocate the right workload: there is an optimal balance point between boredom and anxiety. You want people who feel a real challenge, but one that they believe they can achieve.

Give team members the freedom to plan their own work within the framework of the agreed outcomes, priorities, and schedule. Great teams do not need to be micro-managed.

Do not assume that conflict is a bad sign. Encourage disagreements to surface as something natural to discuss and resolve, rather than as problems to avoid. Resolve team issues like any other issue on a project: do not shy away from them.

There is a definite advantage to co-located, dedicated teams. This enables people to really work as a team, to come together to discuss and resolve problems, and to spark off each other's creativity. This is not always possible, but do not just accept it is impossible – do whatever you can to bring the team together to work together full time in the same location (for tips on geographically dispersed teams see p. 60).

There are thousands of books, blogs and training courses on developing winning teams. Invest some time in them. The rewards in terms of better performance will justify this.

Sustaining the team

When you have built the perfect team, the job is not over. The team must be sustained. This is especially important on long-term projects, where team members leave and new people join. Keep on giving clarity on outcomes, roles, behaviours and project mechanics to both old and new members of the team.

As projects progress the pressure changes. Good intentions can be lost as the project meets high-pressure times, and yet these times are when it is most important to keep focused on good team behaviour, which will lead to productivity.

Reinforce the behaviour you want. The project manager and sponsor should act as role models for the rest of the team, acting as its central components.

Observe and learn as the team works. A high-performance team should not simply be regarded as a way to achieve project outcomes – it is an ideal learning opportunity. Try to capture how the team works, their approaches and tools, their behaviour and styles of interactions. You want to use these again on future projects.

Disbanding the team

Prepare for disbanding the team. For the highest performing teams this can be a painful experience. I do not exaggerate when I say that working on the highest performing teams can be a life-changing experience. People do not like it when this ends. Think it through and mark it with some kind of formal end: time to say farewell and perhaps a final dinner together.

Project manager's checklist

- The success of a project can be eased and speeded up with a high-performance team

- Such a team will not just happen, but needs active management to create

- Ideally, the project manager and sponsor understand high-performance teams and work together to create and sustain such a team

Global and offshore teams

What is this about and why is it important?

More and more projects use resources globally. Offshore suppliers are an increasingly important part of many projects, especially IT projects. Globalisation and improvements in communications technology make worldwide teams a cost-effective way of delivering projects. If anything, this trend is increasing.

How does this impact project managers? Read any of the major *project management* methods or *bodies of knowledge*, and you will find little which cannot be applied to globally based teams. Yet remote and offshore teams create specific challenges for project managers. In this section, I explore these challenges and suggest ways to mitigate them.

Objective

■ To provide tips on how to manage global and offshore project teams to facilitate successful project delivery

Common issues in achieving this objective

→ Treating local and offshore team members the same

→ Assuming that team members from different cultures work and think in the same way

→ Insufficient preparation for the challenges of global teams

The guide

One way to understand the challenges of globally distributed teams or offshore projects is to think about an ideal project. Ask yourself – what are the characteristics of an ideal project? A brainstorming session with a few colleagues is a good way to do this. Soon you will have a list of characteristics for your perfect project. You might find items listed such as effective sponsorship, limited and well-controlled change, sufficient dedicated resources and so forth. Analyse each of these characteristics – many are hard to achieve with global or offshore projects. Offshoring has proven its value, but it is a distinct project environment and poses various challenges for project managers.

There are six main ways global projects differ from locally based projects. Let us look at each of these and discuss what can be done.

Communications

A global team cannot help but have poorer communications than a well-functioning, physically co-located team. If you are working next to someone, dialogue is frequent and instantaneous. When a problem arises you quickly become aware of it, and can rapidly start working out resolutions. The better you understand the status of a project and the sooner you are aware of issues, the better placed you are to manage the project actively. If you are delayed in finding out about a problem, you have less time to resolve it before it impacts project timelines. Although modern technology makes communication easy and possible, rarely is the interaction with an offshore team as immediate or interactive as with a local team.

The answer is to work as closely as possible with your offshore team to minimise delays in communication and to maximise intimacy. If you have an offshore supplier delivering for you, no doubt you will have periodic conference calls set up. These may be essential, but they should not be the only dialogue. Try to make dialogue regular and continuous. Keep calls and instant messenger systems going – if costs are an issue, there are cheap solutions like Skype. Encourage continuous dialogue across the project team, and try not to make all communication through fixed meetings.

Relationships

A result of impaired communications is that relationships are harder to develop. There are many factors that contribute to building relationships, and communications are central. The relationships you build are largely developed from what and how you communicate. Most of us develop better and deeper relationships with those we are in close proximity to and communicate regularly with.

Relationships are central to project management. You can manage people with whom you have a limited relationship, but it is a lot easier when you have a deeper relationship. Someone who has a positive relationship with you is more likely to be honest about progress, issues, *risks* and concerns, and is likely to update you to problems more quickly. They are also more likely to go that extra mile when it is required.

How can you resolve this? Again, one key aspect is to try to ensure you deepen your communications and make them regular. There is no doubt that relationships are usually better with people who talk more often and about a broader range of topics. If possible try and bring the team physically together at least once. This is often not economically viable, but for large *programmes*, the cost of a few flights will be recouped from greater productivity, better understanding and generally more open relationships.

Verifying progress

If a team is remote, progress tends to become harder to track and verify. If your project requires you to manage someone sitting next to you designing a new product it is relatively straightforward to determine how far they have got. If they are thousands of miles away this is difficult. Additionally, as many offshore deliverables are relatively intangible, like bits of software, you will often find that the only measure of progress you have is what your offshore partner tells you.

This is not ideal for project managers, and is made worse if you have little or no relationship with that team or supplier. Finding ways of converting vague supplier statements of progress into tangible milestones is vital. Otherwise, as project manager all you become is a channel for reporting what the supplier has told you and this is hardly value adding.

Power and influence

With an offshore supplier the power of the project manager is generally reduced. This might seem a surprising conclusion for some. Surely your power is inherent in the contract and the possibility of contractually based sanctions? Technically, yes, but calling on the contract should always be a last resort. Frequent reference to the contract is an indicator of a troublesome project. If every time you deal with your offshore supplier you have to refer to the contract, conversations become stilted. Many details of a project need debate and consensus, especially with deliverables like software. Requirements are often ambiguous. You will not get your way if you rely purely on pummelling your offshore supplier with contract terms. You have to influence them. Many effective project managers are used to having little formal power and rely on influence. Distributed projects extend the need for strong influencing skills.

Culture and languages

Different languages are an obvious barrier. Even people speaking nominally the same language, like English, can use terminology in different ways. It is important to take time to remove ambiguities and ensure clarity.

Differences in culture are a notorious trap whilst working internationally. The most useful advice is to work with people who have experience of each other's culture. If this is not possible, try and do your homework and find out about the culture, and tread carefully and sensitively. Some management styles can seem rude and insensitive in some cultures; on the other hand in some countries plain speaking, even bluntness, is essential.

Inconsistent *assumptions* create problems. Different organisations, different countries and different cultures lead to diverse assumptions. This is a major source of project risk. Try and make all assumptions explicit.

It is people who deliver projects, and project management is, in the end, a form of people management. With offshore projects many of the biggest issues are related to people management challenges. Managing people you have never met, who have different working practices and diverse motivations is demanding. If you are sensitive to these issues they can be resolved. Work hard to ensure communications are continuous, do what you can to build relationships, use your influencing skills effectively and most of the challenge can be overcome.

Logistics and legals

There are the logistical issues of working across time zones. For a structured project manager these should not be insurmountable. The challenge is to try and find time slots when everyone can talk. This is possible for some time zones, but once a truly global team is involved it almost always means some late evenings or early mornings for team members. Do not overdo this – but occasionally it is worth the pain to get everyone talking together.

Contracts, especially those created for different legal jurisdictions, can be a maze. It is best to leave this up to professionals, but ensure that they have taken practical delivery considerations into account.

Project manager's checklist

- Compared to a team working in one location, in global projects or those with offshore teams:
  - communications may be inhibited
  - relationships are harder to develop
  - the ability to check and confirm progress is limited
  - the power of the project manager is restricted

- culture and linguistic differences are a source of risk
- logistics and legal issues need to be worked out carefully

▨ With care and planned effort these challenges can be overcome

The effective sponsor

What is this about and why is it important?

Projects must be linked into an organisation's management hierarchy. Without this link they will not gain access to resources, have a mandate and be able to do the things the project needs to do. These links are usually provided by project *sponsors*. Typically, project managers are dependent on sponsors' power, authority and influencing skills.

Effective project sponsorship is an important aspect of successful projects. Unfortunately, many sponsors do not fully understand the requirements of the role and make poor sponsors. This section describes the role, and gives some advice to project managers on how to help their sponsor be an effective one.

Objectives

- To explain the role of the project sponsor
- To encourage project managers to help sponsors to be effective

Common issues in achieving these objectives

- Lack of understanding of how to sponsor projects
- Too little emphasis on the need for good project sponsorship
- Unwillingness on the project manager's behalf to coach sponsors

The guide

The main elements of the project sponsor's role are to:

- identify the business need for a project;
- act as an evangelist for the project;

- provide senior support to a project during execution, especially help with accessing resources, overcoming problems, making decisions and communicating about and retaining support for the project;
- set the business context for a project;
- ensure that the project manager is managing in a competent fashion;
- take accountability for delivery of business benefits.

Such a list is helpful, but the needs of projects vary. Project sponsors' roles must adapt to the unique characteristics of the situation. There are four core factors in this adaptation:

1 the specific needs of a project;
2 the relationship between the project manager and sponsor and how they see their respective roles;
3 the role, level of engagement and skills of other *stakeholders*;
4 the personality, style and availability of the project sponsor.

Making it real

Sponsors pursue their responsibilities in different ways with varying degrees of effectiveness. Project managers must adapt their style and responsibilities in response to sponsor behaviour. This requires assessing sponsors and talking to them. Options should be explored to determine:

- **What needs to be done:** what are the main activities that need to be done by the sponsor and the project manager?
- **What do I do – what do you do:** how does the work split between the project manager and the sponsor?

This should be formalised into a *RACI chart*. More important than the documented RACI chart itself are the understanding and relationship formed in developing it.

The role of the sponsor and the project manager are not constants that can be exhaustively defined in a fixed specification. Each project is unique. It needs a sponsor who will provide the type of sponsorship that is required for that project in its specific situation.

The project manager and sponsor are a double act. They jointly deliver the project, but they are individuals with distinctive ways of working. Project managers who expect sponsors to work in textbook fashion are usually disappointed. Yes, start with generic lists of needs and responsibilities, but be prepared to apply them flexibly.

Helping the project sponsor

Project managers want sponsors who give enough space to get on with the job without constant interference, but they also want sponsors who are there immediately when needed. They like decisive sponsors, who ensure important authorisations are given without delay. It is also appreciated when sponsors are explicit in their praise.

You will come across terrible sponsors: micro-managers, unavailable sponsors, indecisive sponsors and those who respond negatively to everything the project does. Sometimes, it can seem as if the battle is lost at the start of the project! If you find yourself with a poor sponsor, ask yourself: does the sponsor know how to sponsor the project?

Does the sponsor know what to do?

For a project manager there is training, accreditation, books, websites, blogs, etc. to learn from. In contrast, most project sponsors have to work out what being a sponsor means. There is information available on being a project sponsor, but for many senior managers being a project sponsor is a peripheral part of their role. You may be a professional project manager: they are not professional sponsors.

It is easy to assume that sponsors know what being a sponsor means, or to think it is their job to find out. But it is projects that suffer from bad sponsorship and it is in the project manager's interest to help sponsors to understand and do their job properly.

There is an art to helping someone more senior. Generally, senior managers do not respond well to 'Do you know how to do your job?' or 'You must do this and this'. But the same can be achieved by providing clear structures, jointly working through RACI charts, making repeated suggestions and holding regular conversations. Subtle flattery often helps!

Helping sponsors

At the project's start, walk your sponsor through the project plan and point out when you will need their input and decisions made. Set the expectation that projects never go like clockwork and you may need their help on an *ad hoc* basis. Help them to realise there is regular work for them to do.

Book a series of meetings in the sponsor's diary. Do this early in the project for the length of the project, plus a bit for contingency. No-one minds having meetings cancelled out of their diary if they are not required. Fitting one in when you are desperate for help can be difficult. I always start a project by arranging a fixed, once-a-week meeting with the sponsor. You may find that often it is cancelled – but when you need it, it is there.

Develop an understanding of your sponsor's expectations in terms of working style. You must be willing to flex your style to theirs: do not expect them to flex to yours. Work out, or simply ask the sponsor, what the best way to work together is. Alternatively, ask their line reports or other project managers how best to interact with the sponsor.

Getting help

If you need your sponsor's help try to be clear about why you need it. Why is it not possible to solve the issue yourself? Often the answer is obvious, but be prepared to explain it. Be specific and clear in any requests for help: 'I need your help to do ...', 'I cannot do this myself because ...', 'An ideal outcome for the project would be ...'.

Senior managers hate being asked to make a complicated and important decision without advanced warning or time to think about it. Try to warn your sponsors in advance of big decisions coming up, for example, 'Next week I will need help with ...'.

Sometimes advanced warning is not possible – emergencies happen on projects. If you have set your sponsor's expectation that you may need decisions rapidly, then this conversation is easier than if the request for help is a surprise.

See things from their perspective

Most sponsors are busy people and your project is one thing amongst many they are working on. What do they want from you? They want the confidence that everything is under control. You need to deliver, keep them informed and make sure that if a problem arises they are the first to know. But they also want to know that when you use their time it is worthwhile. If you escalate every problem to a sponsor you are not doing your job as a project manager. On the other hand, if you wait until disaster looms to involve them, you are increasing project *risk*.

Manage hands-off sponsors by regularly involving them in decisions and debates about the project. Manage micro-managing sponsors by giving them confidence you know what is going on with accurate, regular updates. Make sure you are their trusted source of information and they are not getting better status updates from anywhere else.

Make it feel as if it is in their interest to be a good sponsor. Play to their egos a bit. Statements of the form, 'I need your expert help in this area ...', 'This is something that needs a senior viewpoint on ...', usually help. Most senior managers and executives are capable and willing to be good sponsors: sometimes they just need a little help.

Project manager's checklist

- Effective sponsorship is essential for successful project delivery

- Unfortunately, some managers are poor sponsors

- Project managers can mitigate this problem by helping their sponsors to understand and perform the role

---

case study

Helping a senior sponsor

Peter is a programme manager *who works on a variety of technology* programmes *in the telecoms and media sectors. His central expertise is in delivering new products. He talks about his experience of coaching project sponsors.*

'On the programmes I am responsible for, I like to think that the sponsor and I are a team. Between us we have to make the programme work and deliver successfully.

'I have had the privilege to work with some brilliant sponsors from whom I have learned a lot. But sometimes the sponsors I work with, whilst being senior leaders in the organisation, do not fully understand the role of being a sponsor. Therefore part of my job is to help them in doing what they need to do. It's not surprising I suppose, as all I do is run programmes, whereas most of my sponsors are senior managers and directors who have lots of other things to do as well as running the programme.

'All the sponsors I have worked with want programmes they sponsor to be successful. The secret to helping someone at a senior level, who wants to be successful, is trust. I can't work with people who know nothing about me and just tell them what to do, especially as they are often more senior than I am. So, when I work with a programme sponsor I have not worked with before, my first goal is to develop trust.

'How do I do this? That's simple. I just get on and do my job reliably and well. I also try to make sure I'm always the first to tell my sponsor any important news about the programme – whether good or bad. I manage their expectations and make sure there are no surprises. When a sponsor sees that you are a safe pair of hands who can be trusted, who is on top of their work, and who is the main source of honest information about the programme, then trust develops.

'When your sponsor trusts you, you can start to suggest things: "It might be appropriate if you …", "It would be good if …" Quite quickly this can become the normal way of working.'

A productive stakeholder community

What is this about and why is it important?

One of the biggest bugbears of many project teams is dealing with *stakeholders*. The effort entailed in managing them can be considerable. In the worst situation, interactions with a project's stakeholder community are a continuous, counter-productive battle. Stakeholders may micro-manage, interfere, ignore the project's needs, be indecisive, keep changing the project's direction, lack consensus, openly mistrust or disregard the project team and so forth. *Stakeholder management* is then a painful and seemingly pointless overhead on the project. Yet it does not need to be like this. In the best situation, stakeholders actively contribute to the project's success. What causes the difference?

There is an element of luck in the stakeholders a project has. Sometimes you just get awful and difficult stakeholders. But the behaviour of stakeholders can be moderated and positively improved by the project team's actions. On the other hand, inappropriate or poorly perceived behaviour by the project team can turn even the most supportive stakeholders into the project's enemies. Stakeholder management is thus an important project task.

Objectives

- To ensure a productive relationship with a stakeholder community
- To make stakeholders into a proactive resource for the project

Common issues in achieving these objectives

→ Treating stakeholder management as a low-priority activity, resulting in insufficient effort on stakeholder management

→ Not planning stakeholder management, hence insufficient resource and time are available to perform it

→ Lack of clarity of responsibilities for stakeholder management

→ Inability or unwillingness to see things from the stakeholders' perspective

The guide

The goal

In order to achieve a productive stakeholder relationship be clear about the characteristics of an ideal relationship. Of course it is not always, or even often, possible to achieve such an ideal relationship. But by having this as a target you set the direction to aim for.

In the ideal situation:

- Stakeholders actively support the project, removing roadblocks and providing resources.
- Project team members understand the stakeholders' perspectives, needs, priorities and constraints clearly.
- Stakeholders are willing to do tasks on behalf of the project, working as an extended resource pool to be drawn upon.
- Stakeholders have a good understanding of project capabilities and demand a realistic set of outcomes, being willing to drop nice-to-have, peripheral and unrelated requirements. The aim is usually *not* to fulfil every single requirement of every stakeholder. This leads to over-engineered solutions. The aim is to quickly deliver the essentials at low *risk*.
- Stakeholders understand the sort of behaviour that helps projects and what hinders them and are willing to take guidance from the project manager as to what to do.

▦ The project team have the capability to satisfy the stakeholders.

To achieve this requires the right attitude and approach to managing stakeholders.

Developing a productive stakeholder relationship

The starting point for a productive stakeholder relationship is to know who the stakeholders are. It may seem obvious, but it can be a challenge to identify all the relevant stakeholders. There is a balance to be found, as only so many stakeholders can be managed. A project manager who considers the *sponsor* as the only stakeholder is being naive. But a project with a list of hundreds of stakeholders to individually manage is unrealistic and will not lead to productive stakeholder management.

The number of stakeholders who should be managed varies between types of projects. A complex organisational change normally needs to manage far more stakeholders than a pure technical development. Stakeholders can be organised into groups with those with similar needs and characteristics. A project team then interacts with a group representative. The most effective stakeholder management actions are tailored to individuals. However, the most efficient is to group stakeholders into as small a number of groups as possible. Again, a balance needs to be found.

Once you have identified your stakeholders and stakeholder groups, analyse them and their needs. What specific actions you need to take depend on the situation, but in general:

▦ Engage and interact with stakeholders. Stakeholder management is not a theoretical exercise and cannot be achieved by the project team working in an office without talking to stakeholders.

▦ Make the process for interaction explicit and agreed with the stakeholders. Try to avoid undertaking stakeholder management as an *ad hoc* activity.

- Manage them and their expectations, trying to avoid surprises. It is much better to give bad news early than to surprise with it late in the project. Build trust by keeping to commitments and by being open.
- Take time to educate stakeholders on how they can help the project to deliver effectively and efficiently.
- Make clear that a successful project needs stakeholders to do things, as well as present requirements and needs to the project team.
- Try to give something back to the stakeholders, so they see the value of active engagement.

Focus on both the stakeholders who support the project and those who are less helpful. Ignoring either of the groups adds risks and can lead to unaligned project *objectives* and direction.

From the project team's perspective, plan stakeholder engagement and management as a core project task. It should not be an add-on activity that gets done as and when there is time. Manage your own and the team's expectations: stakeholder management is an important task that time and resource needs to be allocated to. It is not a peripheral 'fluffy' activity, but a central pillar of project success.

Whose responsibility?

If stakeholder management is to be undertaken, someone needs to have responsibility for it; it must not fall into the gaps between project roles.

In most projects, responsibility for stakeholder management sits with the project manager and project sponsor. I am always wary of shared responsibilities. An important and early discussion between the project manager and project sponsor should be to agree and ideally document who has to do what with regard to which stakeholders. For complex *programmes*, allocating dedicated resources in the project team to stakeholder management may be required.

In an *agile* project, the situation is clearer. Stakeholder management is a responsibility of the product owner.

Additional benefits of effective stakeholder management

Stakeholder management is often presented as a way of understanding needs and of avoiding potential project problems. These are important reasons to perform stakeholder management, but there are other benefits:

- Proactive stakeholders effectively provide an extended team of additional resources (for free!).
- Good stakeholder management reduces some risks and makes other risks, which may otherwise be unnoticed, transparent.
- It increases the likelihood of a project being perceived as a success. Irrespective of actual project outcome, stakeholders who have been engaged and whose expectations have been managed are far likelier to perceive a project as a success than those who have been ignored.
- It eases *benefits realisation* and the transition phase at the end of a project when deliverables are handed over to their owners.

Good stakeholder management really shows its value when projects have to implement change, especially if that change is contentious. Involving stakeholders as early as possible in a project is a significant contribution towards sustained change. Ignoring them always makes change much harder, and sometimes impossible.

Project manager's checklist

- Stakeholder management is an important activity on a project, which needs to be planned and have adequate time and resources allocated to it to perform effectively

- Make responsibilities for stakeholder management explicit

- Good stakeholder management increases the likelihood of projects being perceived as a success, and eases benefits realisation and implementing change

four

Delivering the project

The first three parts of book were concerned with building and acquiring everything you need to run the project. In this part, we switch to the application of those various tools, resources, relationships and plans. The whole reason for building the project structure is to enable delivery. This part discusses delivery, the central aspect of project management.

People tend to think in terms of activities, and project plans are usually defined in terms of tasks or activities. But the project team must not just do things – the tasks being done have to lead to the desired outcomes. This is discussed in the first section. The second section looks at the range of knowledge project managers need to manage delivery successfully. The third section explores project risk and how you can handle it. Finally, we look at project reporting and how you can ensure it is value adding. Reporting is the bane of many project managers' lives, getting in the way of delivery – whereas it should be a valuable aid to delivery.

Managing progress: perform, deliver, accomplish

What is this about and why is it important?

A project manager's main goal on a day-to-day basis is to ensure projects progress. The daily work involved in this has many aspects: monitoring, chasing, resolving issues, avoiding *risks*, motivating teams, giving instructions, updating documentation, communicating, making decisions, taking control by making appropriate interventions, liaising with *stakeholders* and so on. Two of these aspects are most central to managing progress: monitoring and control.

Monitoring is concerned with regularly assessing the progress of the project and comparing it with the expected status as defined in the plan. Ideally progress matches the plan, but there is often a variance between plans and reality – the project is off track.

Control is concerned with making deliberate and appropriate interventions in the project when the project is off track, or when the plan and approach can be enhanced. The latter occurs as understanding improves and lessons are learned during the project's progress. Then the approach can be improved and progressively elaborated.

Objectives

- To understand project monitoring
- To appreciate when interventions are required to keep a project on track
- To ensure progress is leading to the desired deliverables and outcomes

Common issues in achieving these objectives

➤ Poor planning

➤ Ineffective progress monitoring

➤ Inappropriate interventions

➤ Monitoring activity without linking it to outcomes

The guide

Earlier, I described a process of translation used in planning (see p. 33) that went:

Objectives ⟶ Deliverables ⟶ Task

This translation was done to understand how to achieve a desired effect (accomplishing *objectives*) by implementing its causes (performing tasks). One way to think of progress management is as an inversion of this translation. In monitoring a project, the project manager is mainly focusing on activity: what are the project team members doing and is this as defined in the plan? Additionally, the project manager should ensure this activity is leading to the desired outcome. Progress monitoring goes from cause to effect.

My inversion uses verbs rather than nouns, because it represents the active process of delivery:

Perform tasks ⟶ Deliver deliverables ⟶ Accomplish objectives

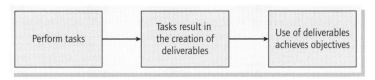

The process of delivery

The project manager should confirm that:

- **The plan is being followed:** the project team members are performing the tasks allocated to them in the time and budget estimated.
- **There were no gaps or overlaps in the *decomposition*:** all the necessary tasks are in the plan, and only the necessary tasks are in the plan.
- **The original translation was accurate:** the tasks being performed are progressing to the creation of the expected deliverables and the accomplishment of the anticipated objectives.

In reality, translations and decompositions are always imperfect. In monitoring and controlling, the project manager seeks to learn and improve the plan as the project progresses. As mentioned earlier (see p. 39) plans are never perfect – they evolve.

Monitoring progress

To monitor progress effectively, you must do it frequently. At the same time, if you want a motivated and highly performing project team, monitoring needs to be done so that they do not feel they are being micro-managed (see p. 55). The balance is found when the project team understands why the project manager must monitor progress frequently, and the project manager respects the team's need to work without constant nagging. A good team accepts regular progress reviews – even on a daily basis, when it helps the team to accomplish their objectives.

Additionally, good progress monitoring is not just about asking people what they have done, it seeks evidence and builds in quality reviews of work and outputs (see p. 122).

The frequency of review varies and depends on the scale, urgency and complexity of a project. I prefer frequent reviews, as they can be short and simple. Additionally, regular reviews quickly highlight variances between reality and the plan. The earlier a variance is identified, the easier it is to resolve.

A typical process with indicative timings is as follows:

- Check that tasks are being done (frequency: daily to weekly).
- Reflect on whether the tasks are resulting in progress towards the development of deliverables (frequency: weekly to monthly).
- Check that the tasks being done and deliverables produced remain in *scope* (frequency: weekly to monthly).
- Reflect on whether progress is being made towards the achievement of objectives (frequency: monthly to quarterly).

All the team should be continuously and consciously aware of objectives. When they make any project choices or decisions, they should ask themselves – does that help towards accomplishing objectives?

Linking performance to accomplishment

There are activities within many projects to ensure the right and complete deliverables are produced – called *testing*. The achievement of objectives is assessed through *benefits tracking* (see p. 166).

Testing and benefits tracking are effective disciplines, but they are done once deliverables are produced or objectives are meant to have been achieved. This is usually too late to take easy, quick and cheap correcting action when a project is off track. Problems in deliverables and meeting objectives found at the end of a project are usually complex and expensive to resolve.

Hence, project managers should frequently assess whether the project is going in the right direction towards producing the expected deliverables and accomplishing the desired outcomes. Such an assessment is usually subjective and judgemental, but is still important.

Interventions

There is no point in monitoring progress unless it results in action. Monitoring enables progress reporting, but that is a side-effect. The main purpose is to enable appropriate interventions to be taken to keep the project on track or to amend it in some way.

There is no fixed list of controlling actions a project manager should take, it depends on the situation. *Project management* practices, processes and tools show when interventions are required, but they do not determine what those interventions should be. That is up to the skill, creativity, experience and insight of the project manager.

However, it is possible to identify the main generic categories of interventions a project manager can make (in a rough order of increasing seriousness):

- nothing – let the project carry on as is, but keep monitoring (this is the right option in many situations);
- alter the allocation or prioritisation of work amongst project team members;
- tweak the plan or approach;
- escalate to *sponsor* or other stakeholders for help;
- release contingency;
- raise a *change request*;
- change team members;

- seek additional resources;
- revise the scope or objectives;
- radically revise the approach;
- stop the project (rare, but occasionally necessary).

Challenges

I have presented a logical structure for managing project progress. All of it depends on monitoring, but in practice project managers frequently have a poor understanding of status. This typically arises when monitoring occurs too infrequently, in insufficient detail, without seeking evidence or when responsibilities for task completion are unclear.

Additionally, even when task status is well understood, it is not uncommon for project managers to be unaware whether the tasks are leading to the expected deliverables or to accomplishing the desired objectives. This is usually because the project manager is focusing on the task – and forgets to review deliverables, or more commonly objective accomplishment. A detailed focus on progress in completing tasks is to be praised – as long as it is not at the cost of losing sight of why the project is being done, i.e. losing sight of the objectives.

All sorts of issues and risks may surface during a project. But from a monitoring perspective the main issues, in increasing order of seriousness, are:

- **Incomplete tasks breakdown due to poor decomposition or translation from deliverables:** this is a regular occurrence. Understanding improves as the project's progress and tasks need to be revisited. This problem must be minimised, but happens to some extent on all projects.
- **Forgotten/wrong deliverables due to poor translation from objectives or bad design:** hopefully forgetting deliverables is rare, although some individual requirements are often missed out. It is best if this is identified and resolved early. If recognised only late in a project's *lifecycle* it can be difficult, expensive and time consuming to resolve.

■ **Incorrect or incomplete objectives due to poor analysis of business needs:** this is serious! It may be resolved if the required alteration is small and identified quickly. But if it is significant, it may be best to abandon the project.

Project manager's checklist

■ Progress management is the core day-to-day task of project managers

■ It consists of monitoring progress towards the completion of tasks, and taking appropriate interventions when progress is off track

■ Project managers must ensure task progress is resulting in the development of the expected deliverables and in the accomplishment of the desired objectives

What project managers need to know

What is this about and why is it important?

What knowledge is required by project managers to deliver projects? I group the knowledge into three categories. The first category is the core skills of *project management* such as planning and managing *risks*. These are the **process and practices** of project management. The second category involves specialist knowledge of the type of project – whether it is developing an IT system, designing a car, building a bridge or creating a new product, etc. This is the **content** of a project. Finally, there is knowledge of the environment in which projects are run – such as the culture of the organisation and country in which the project is run. This is the **context** of a project.

This section looks at process and practice, content and context knowledge.

Objectives

- To explain the types of knowledge that project managers need
- To understand how to develop and be able to apply this knowledge

Common issues in achieving these objectives

→ Focus on process and practice knowledge to the exclusion of content and context knowledge

→ Relying solely on 'on-the-job' learning to acquire knowledge

The guide

Process and practices

The core knowledge required by project managers covers the processes, techniques, tools and practices of project management. This is the knowledge required to perform the role of the project manager as described earlier (see p. 14). This includes knowledge of scoping, planning, estimating, *risk* and issue *management*, progress control, *stakeholder management* and project team management. It also includes knowledge of associated tools such as planning and resource management tools.

Although this book does not go into detail there are extensions of project management in *programme* and *portfolio management* which some project managers need knowledge of as well.

Process and practice knowledge is what is typically taught on project management courses, and is associated with project management accreditations. The degree of knowledge required depends on the scale, complexity and risk of a project.

Content

The project manager's role is to manage the tasks on a project, not to do them. The doing is done by the project team. As a result, one ongoing debate concerns how much content knowledge project managers need. Do IT project managers need to be experts in IT, or civil engineering project managers experts in building?

This conversation tends to be dominated by extreme views: either yes, the project manager must be an expert, or no, the project manager needs to know nothing about the content of the project. The truth lies between the two extremes.

The project manager does not need to be a content expert, but does need to know sufficient about the content of the project. 'Sufficient' is an ambiguous word. In reality, the level of content knowledge varies from situation to situation. So how can you determine what sufficient is?

The project manager must be able to converse productively with experts on the project team, to probe what they say and to look for gaps. This requires some understanding of the jargon and concepts the expert team members use. The project manager has to integrate the planning inputs from different members of the project team. This requires some understanding of what the activities are. The project manager must control the process of delivery. This requires an ability to make judgements about task progress and completeness of deliverables. The project manager must be able to get experts to identify and manage the project risks. Project risks are not generic to all projects, but are specific to individual projects.

This points to a need for a good understanding of the content of the project, whilst not necessarily being a deep expert in every aspect. For example, a project manager working in civil engineering or construction would expect to understand contracts, contract negotiation, and managing sub-contractors; an IT project manager often needs to be able to manage offshore teams; and a project manager in new product development needs familiarity with marketing and sales. Yet what each of these project managers regards as core, the others may have no knowledge of.

Project managers *may* be content experts, but if they are their role on the project is not to be the content expert. Having deep content knowledge can be very helpful – as long as project managers remember their role is to project manage not deliver the content of the project.

Context

Projects run within an environment which varies from project to project. Organisations have different cultures, and successful project managers must operate well within that specific culture.

An understanding of organisational culture requires sensitivity to the characteristics of individual organisations. How are decisions made? How do things really get done? What are the right and wrong ways of getting *sponsor* support? What sort of behavioural expectations does the organisation have? And so on.

There could be advantages in not being immersed in an organisation's culture. Sometimes outsiders can overcome the problems associated with sticking with the 'way things are done around here'. Creative innovation often requires an outsider's viewpoint.

It is not just organisational culture that matters, national culture does as well. I have worked in nine countries and the cultures varied significantly. In one country the culture is very command and control orientated. Nothing is done without formal mandate and explicit permission from senior managers. In another, work progresses only when there is consensus. In a third, delivery works best by informal mechanisms and relationships outside the formal management hierarchy. Multinational projects add yet more complexity (see p. 60). Assuming techniques that work in one culture will work in another culture is a fast way to a failing project.

Project managers need some degree of context skills – or the flexibility and adaptability to change their style of working to make best use of the organisation and culture in which they work.

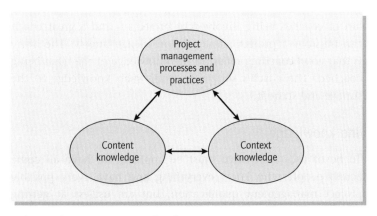

What project managers need to know

Developing knowledge

So how should project managers develop this knowledge? The most obvious way is to get involved in projects and learn by doing. As a practical skill, there is little better way to learn than by doing. However, such on-the-job learning can be haphazard and is best supported by other mechanisms.

As an author I am bound to encourage reading. Project managers benefit by reading around the subject and keeping up to date on trends in the discipline, but only so much can be learned by reading alone.

There are many project management training courses available which offer specific approaches and techniques and a formal qualification. As the profession progresses such formal qualifications are becoming more essential. The best training courses do not simply push information out, but allow plenty of time for discussion between practitioners. Often the most valuable learning comes from other practitioners facilitated by the trainer, rather than from the trainer's words.

Much of the best learning comes from practical experience combined with time to review and reflect on projects, and consciously adapt approaches based on experiences. I am a big fan of coaches being involved in projects – and a great coach can improve a project manager's knowledge hugely. The irony is that good coaching relies on the knowledge of the team being coached. The coach's skill is to bring such knowledge to the surface and share it.

Applying knowledge

To be of use, knowledge must be applied. We have all come across people who know everything and have every possible project management qualification, but are useless at getting anything done. This is because applying knowledge in projects relies on a set of personal and inter-personal behaviours, traits and skills. Included in this are characteristics such as: being a good listener and analyst, being structured, being decisive, making good judgements, being persuasive and motivational, taking ownership for the projects, being progress driven and outcome focused (see pp. 55, 136 and 249). More information is also contained in Chapters 2, 4 and 6 of my book *The Project Manager: Mastering the Art of Delivery* (Pearson Education, 2010).

Such characteristics can be greatly improved by good coaching and the example of one's peers, managers and leaders.

Project manager's checklist

■ Project managers need to have process and practice knowledge – along with some content and context knowledge

■ There are various sources of this knowledge: on-the-job learning, training, coaching and reading. Ideally a combination is used

■ To be of value the project manager must be capable of applying this knowledge productively

---

case study

Understanding the project's content

Dave is a consultant project manager. He works for large organisations who are trying to run bigger projects than they normally do, and who consequently need to call on external help for support. Sometimes he is hired as a project manager, on other occasions his role is to build and improve the organisation's project management skills so they can deliver the project themselves. He shares his views on the need for project managers to have content knowledge.

'I have worked in many different industries and on many different projects in my 30 years as a project manager. I like the challenge associated with working in an unfamiliar industry, maybe in a country I have not worked in before, and perhaps with a slightly different sort of project than I have been involved in before.

'I guess I am an advert for the jack-of-all trades sort of project manager. But in truth I cannot run every single type of project. I have to understand a reasonable amount about the type of project I am running. There is no doubt in my mind that I am most comfortable working in situations which I am familiar with – and the more I know about the content of the project before I start, the quicker I am able to add value as a project manager. The picture of the generic project manager who can successfully run any project is, in my view, a myth.

'If I have a good team around me, I am normally able to overcome the problems associated with not knowing about detailed specifics in one area of the project or another. But the more I know about the project, the more I can assist the team, the better I am at predicting and managing risks and issues, and the better I am able to structure the most appropriate project plan.

'One piece of advice, as there is one trap to avoid if you are the project manager and a content expert: always remember you are the project manager and not the deliverable designer, builder, tester or anything else. Your expertise can help to make the project a success, but you must give people in the project team space to get on with their appointed roles, even if you think you could do them better!'

Understanding project risk

What is this about and why is it important?

In Part 1 we discussed the role of project managers and concluded that whilst there are many things that project managers do, there are two basic reasons why we need them. Firstly, projects are complex. They require planning effective and efficient ways to deliver them, and need ongoing co-ordination and management. Secondly, projects are exposed to *risk*. We cannot just plan uncertainty away. Risk must be identified, assessed and dealt with. This is the arena of *risk management*.

It is risk that makes projects challenging and to a large extent interesting. It takes skilled *project management* and experience to deal fully with risk, and risk management is an essential element of delivering a project. The foundation of risk management is an appreciation for and identification of risks.

(This section relates to pp. 108, 122 and 196.)

Objectives

- To appreciate the importance of risk management in successful project delivery
- To assist project teams in identifying risk

Common issues in achieving these objectives

- Insufficient focus on risk by project teams
- Complacency about risk
- Focus on the wrong risks or wrong categories of risk

The guide

There are various definitions of risk and risk management (for those interested see ISO 31000, *APM BoK* or *PMI* BoK). The definitions focus on the potential of actions or events to impact the achievement of project *objectives* – whether positively or negatively. Here I focus on the negative outcomes from risk, but risk management can equally be considered in terms of unexpectedly positive outcomes, otherwise known in project management as *opportunities*.

Classically, in project management there are two key dimensions to project risk: likelihood and impact. The likelihood is the probability that a risk will be realised. The impact is a measure of effect on the project should the risk occur.

The sources of risk

Life is inherently indeterminate. I am not making a philosophical point, but reflecting reality. We do not know everything, and we do not have the time or resources to analyse and assess every possible aspect of a project. Hence we have risk.

There are various sources of risk on projects, which can be summarised into four overlapping groups:

1   *Assumptions*: we make assumptions all the time. Sometimes they are reasonable and turn out to be right, sometimes they are wrong. Risk is associated with the likelihood and impact of wrong assumptions. Project assumptions should be identified and assessed as risks.

2   **Actions, or consequences of actions, impacting the project:** for example the behaviour of *stakeholders* in response to proposed project plans. Stakeholder assessments are a good way to identify risk.

3   **Uncertainties and unknowns:** the more innovative, unusual or experimental a project is, the greater the number of unknowns. Unknowns are hard to manage as individual risks, but can be accounted for in terms of contingency.

Uncertainties include factors such as whether suppliers will deliver on time or whether a project budget will be maintained for the life of the project.

4   **Errors:** human error is a fact of life. In a complex activity like building a project plan it is likely there will be mistakes in some areas.

Additionally, a project is not just exposed to risk, it is a source of risk to other stakeholders and their objectives (e.g. the risk that a project may disrupt business operations).

The categories of risk

Risk is often talked about as if it is one thing, but as pointed out above there are different types of risk. You can also categorise risk to determine the relevance of different risks to customers, stakeholders, *sponsors*, the project manager and project team members. Each risk is relative to an objective or set of objectives – and only those risks that impact objectives that are of interest to specific groups are relevant to those groups (or individuals).

Therefore, what risks are relevant to a project depend on perspective. Project managers need to be clear about what risks they are responsible for, and which they can ignore. But when identifying risks, instead of thinking in black and white terms of what is and is not relevant to a project, risks can be considered as closer or further from the project's objectives. In this way, project risks fall into categories:

- **Project risk:** risks that threaten the project being delivered to time, cost or quality. These are the core risks, directly relevant to and managed by the project manager and team.

- **Outcome risk:** risks that threaten the achievement of the desired outcomes or business benefits from a project. This category extends beyond project risks. These risks are relevant to project sponsors and customers. Project managers are often not responsible for achieving the business benefits from a project and may not be concerned with outcome risks. In contrast, *programme managers* usually are and have to consider outcome risks. (This is one key area where the roles of project and programme managers vary.)

- **Design, architectural or integration risk:** risks that the implementation and use of project deliverables will impact other components of an organisation. For example, a new IT system or new process disrupting existing IT systems or processes. This sort of risk is normally the responsibility of the solutions designer or architect and is identified through design reviews as part of the project.

- **Operational risk:** risks that the running of the project, or implementation of deliverables from it, will disrupt the wider operations of the business, or impact the total cost of ownership of business operations in unforeseen, unbudgeted or unplanned ways. These risks are most relevant to operational managers in an organisation. This is often a point of tension between projects and operational managers.

- **Organisational culture risk:** risks that the project will have an unforeseen or unplanned impact upon the culture or behaviours of people in the organisation. In my experience this is often forgotten, but change projects have significant impacts on the consistency of behaviour in organisations.

- **Social risk:** risks that the project will have a cultural, environmental or ethical impact on the wider community in which an organisation operates. Most projects do not need to consider this, but some, such as launching new products or those with environmental impact should and often do. This is usually the area of corporate social responsibility (CSR) and sometimes statutory regulation and acts.

There is no universal rule as to which risks should and should not be considered. This depends on the context in which the project operates and the nature of the project. Often there is a tension between the interests of different stakeholders, and good *governance* processes should ensure that the project is accounting for all the risks it should account for (see p. 196).

Approaches to risk management

Project managers invest differing amounts of effort in risk management, and often too little. Risk management needs to be an ongoing active part of project management involving all members of a project team (see p. 108 for ways to achieve this).

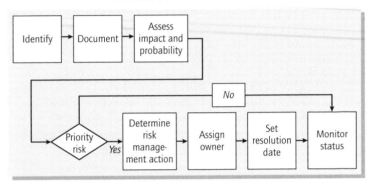

A typical simple risk management process

There are various ways to support the identification of risk. Specific risk identification techniques include brainstorming, stakeholder interviews and root cause analysis. Experience is often the best way to identify relevant risks. If you are involved in running a project in a domain you have no experience of, engaging someone who has run similar projects before in risk identification workshops or interviews is recommended. Additionally, there are many risk management checklists available which can help trigger your thinking on what risks should be considered (for example, see checklists 10.1 and 10.2 in my book *Brilliant Checklists for Project Managers* (Pearson Education, 2012).

For very specialist situations there are advanced and specific risk assessment techniques, such as Monte Carlo simulations. These are only required for very large or most complex of *programmes*.

Project manager's checklist

- Risk is an inherent feature of projects

- Risk management is a core element of project management, and should be an active component of a project

- The foundation of risk management is risk identification

- There are various categories of risk relevant to different objectives

- Project managers should be clear which aspects of risk they are and are not including in their risk management processes, depending on the objectives they are responsible for

Value-added project reporting

What is this about and why is it important?

Reporting is a central part of project delivery. There is a variety of reports to produce: status reports, budget updates, *steering committee* packs and so on. Reporting can take up a significant proportion of project resources, and is often a point of dissatisfaction for project managers, project *sponsors* and other *stakeholders*.

Project reporting causes project sponsors' and project managers' eyes to roll – for different reasons. Sponsors are often unhappy with the reports they get. Project managers are often unhappy about the effort expended in reporting. Sponsors claim they cannot understand what is going on. Project managers complain about drowning in documents and PowerPoint presentations, and being unable to do 'any real work'.

This section looks at a sensible approach to project reporting. An approach that meets the needs of different stakeholders, and adds value without being an excessive overhead.

Objectives

- To determine the right level of project reporting
- To understand the different project reports required

Common issues in achieving these objectives

- Insufficient consideration of the needs of report recipients: why do they need reports and what do they do with them?
- Reporting as habit rather than as a goal-directed activity

The guide

Reporting goals

Badly managed reporting wastes time, but project reports have productive uses. They keep those external to the project informed about the project and able to take whatever decisions and actions they need as a result of the project. Secondly, project teams can use reports to drive the things they need from these external groups, whether that is decision making, resource allocation or any other activities undertaken. Hence we can derive two basic goals in project reporting:

1 Meeting the needs of both project stakeholders and the project itself.

2 Achieving this efficiently and effectively by maximising value from and minimising the overhead of reporting.

By holding these goals in mind we can develop the most value-added reports.

Putting yourself in someone else's shoes

The starting point for value-added reporting is to ask the questions: who is the report for, and what do they need from the report? A report is not just meant to reflect what the report writer has to say, but is a tool to help the reader make judgements and decisions, and take the right actions.

When thinking about project reports, try to put yourself in the shoes of the person reading it and understand what they want. On top of this, a report is also a tool for the writer to get the things done they want done.

There is potentially a large range of different audiences for project reports, but we can simplify them into two: interested external parties in a project, known as stakeholders, and the project and project team itself. Their needs are conceptually simple.

■ Stakeholder needs are:
    - to understand progress towards achieving goals;

- to ensure their needs are being met by the project;
- to prepare for any decisions or actions they need to take as a result of the project.

■ Project team needs are:

- to manage stakeholder expectations, maintain their awareness of project team performance, and develop their confidence in the project;
- to highlight *risks* and issues stakeholders should be aware of, or need to take action over;
- to facilitate decision making and approvals by sponsors and stakeholders;
- to gain and maintain access to resources and prioritisation.

Test every report you write: is it giving stakeholders what they need, is it helping you to achieve your goals? Or put more simply: are you informing appropriately and making the right requests? Only when you answer yes to both parts of this question is it a good report.

Reporting principles

Project management is not reporting, but an element of reporting is essential to all projects. This must either be done by the project manager or delegated to another party, such as the *project management office (PMO)*.

The style and volume of reporting required should vary depending on the needs and context of the project. For example reports may have to scale up or down to account for the size, complexity, risk, value and visibility of the project.

Projects managers should aim to be able to produce reports quickly and simply. If the project manager cannot quickly report status, the likelihood is that they are not on top of the project.

Ideally, reporting should be a natural outcome of the project work being done. For this to happen project work products and artefacts need to be designed so that they can be presented to wider audiences. In reality, there is usually some need to tailor to specific audiences, but this should be minimised.

Project managers should seek to minimise reporting overhead. But they must also recognise that it is an important task that adds value. They should recognise that different audiences require different types of information, which may require different reports. The project manager should seek to balance the gains from producing a variety of reports, with the efficiencies from producing as few as possible. A good attitude is to think of developing as many as necessary and as few as possible.

Try to cut out anything that is not adding value, and stop reports that stakeholders have ceased reading. Politics and culture have an impact on this, and it would be naive to think that every project can just ignore the things it does not want to do or does not think adds value.

Designing reports

The appropriate level of reporting is context sensitive. Here are some examples of the factors you need to consider:

- Whether the project is politically contentious or not: contentious projects usually have to do more *stakeholder management* and associated reporting.
- Whether the project operates in a situation with generous or constrained resourcing: when resources are constrained, reporting needs tend to increase to maintain access to resources and appropriate prioritisation.
- Whether the project needs regular support from senior managers (e.g. to take actions, make decisions or give approvals) or is largely self-contained: the more active sponsors and stakeholders need to be, the greater the reporting overhead to steer this activity.
- Whether the culture of the organisation is formal or informal: this is less about the reporting needs and more about the frequency and style of reports. Less formal organisations tend to have regular updates in the form of

conversations. More formal organisations tend to insist on formalised periodic reports.

■ How homogeneous the stakeholders are: when stakeholders have similar needs, levels of understanding and attitudes, one report may satisfy all. If the stakeholder community is varied, the number and range of reports tends to increase.

Finding the balance

Optimising the reports you produce is about balancing a variety of needs and contending pressures. Reports need to be designed for your specific context and requirements. What are the needs of your project, given the environment and context it operates in? This should be taken account of in project planning and resourcing.

When a project is started, the reporting processes, report formats and responsibilities should be defined to meet the needs of the project and its stakeholders. As the project progresses, periodically review the reports to make sure they are reaching the right audiences and enabling groups to make the right decisions, whilst never being afraid to stop reports that have ceased to add value.

This can be challenging when organisations insist on standard templates. But do not reject standard templates out of hand. Firstly, you may have no choice but to use them. Secondly, the reality is that many projects in one organisation face similar pressures, and have to report for similar needs. Standard templates can work, as long as they are well designed for the organisation, and there is flexibility in the level and detail of content input.

Additionally, standard templates may be well received by sponsors as they are familiar with them and know how to extract the right information. However, when you have the situation that a template has to be immensely complex to suit different stakeholder needs, or does not provide the right information for stakeholders, then it is time to redesign them.

Project manager's checklist

- Poorly designed reports can waste considerable time and resources

- Project reporting is essential, and if well designed will add value to stakeholders and the project team

- Reporting needs are context specific, and reporting processes, formats and responsibilities should be well thought through and not done as a matter of habit

Practical project management

The preceding four parts of this book explored some of the essential foundations of project management. In this part I want to build on that, and look at some key lessons from experience. I will look at the factors that differentiate competent project managers from the high performers.

The first section looks again at risk management and how you convert it from being a passive discipline to a core component of a project. The second section discusses an area of efficiency – multi-tasking, and puts the case for reducing it as much as possible. The third section explores the plan on a page. In the era of PowerPoint, the plan on a page has become a standard piece of project management. This can be a powerful communication tool, but can also be misleading. When is it appropriate to use, and when should plans on a page be avoided? Finally, I discuss the issue of helping others in a project team. In doing this, is it better to directly assess, criticise and praise people's work or to act more like a coach?

Making risk management real

What is this about and why is it important?

Risk management is a central pillar of *project management*. If there was no *risk* the life of project managers would be considerably simpler. It would also be a much less skilled job. The inexperienced often see project management as a process of developing a plan and following it. In truth, whilst planning is essential, it is not sufficient to guarantee a smooth project. Risk is inherent in the world. The unexpected will occur and we cannot plan risk away. But we can prepare for risk, and the process by which this is done is risk management.

Risk management is sometimes portrayed as a minor part of project management. It is pursued in a passive 'tick box' style of mentality. Many project teams have fallen into the trap of doing insufficient risk management. Usually at some point on the project something goes wrong. This 'something' was predictable within a range of probabilities, and worse it was often avoidable. If the team had taken the time to do risk management properly they could have predicted the problem, and taken action to avoid it.

Objectives

- To understand the symptoms of poor risk management
- To ensure that risk management is an integral and active part of managing a project
- To know how to make it an active part of the project

Common issues in achieving these objectives

Insufficient understanding of the criticality of risk management

Once-off risk assessment performed at the start of a project which is never updated

→ Risk management performed to achieve compliance to standards, rather than being positively engaged with

→ Lack of encouragement for risk management from *sponsors* and *stakeholders*

The guide

Risk management is one of those aspects of project management that all project managers conceptually understand, but many do not do well enough. I suspect at times many project managers do not give enough focus to risk and know that I have been guilty of this sometimes.

There are different approaches to managing risk. In this section, I do not want to talk about the actual mechanics of identifying or managing risk (see p. 94), but look at the signs that it is not being managed properly and consider ways to make risk management effective.

Typical symptoms of poor risk management

There will be lots of unique factors affecting every project. This means that each project has a unique set of risks. Even so, in general there are a few common symptoms of poor risk management:

▪ **There is no understanding of the risks.** This is a surprisingly common reality for many projects. Ask a group of project managers to tell you the risks on their projects and to see the risk log. Often nothing has been done about risk and managers have difficulty in clearly identifying the key risks.

▪ **There is an old, outdated risk log.** We have all been guilty of this on some projects. Some form of risk assessment is done at the start of the project. Risks are identified, categorised, assessed and some vague words are written down about what to do about them. The log is then filed away and largely forgotten about. Should anyone ask to see the risk log, an old dusty document is produced. It has never been updated since the start of the project! Be honest – you have seen this lots of times.

▪ **There is compliance to risk management, but no action.** This is the hardest to spot, and is a common trait, especially with less capable project managers. A risk management process is defined, is active and a risk log is regularly maintained. Risk review meetings are held, but no real action ever occurs in response to those risks, and everyone looks very bored at the meetings. Risk management is done to achieve compliance to standards, rather than to achieve better project outcomes. In a way this is the worst situation of all, as effort is made, but nothing useful is done.

Making it real

Risk management is included as a project management practice because it adds value, but to add value it needs to be a real live activity. How can you make risk management real? I think there are five fundamental characteristics of a project in which risk management is real:

1 **The project manager has the right mindset.** One of the reasons we need project management in the first place is because of the inherent risk in projects. If there were no risks, we would probably need fewer project managers. The ability to overcome risks is a key trait of great project management. Successful project managers are orientated towards risk, constantly aware of it and alert for new risks. Unless the project manager really believes in the existence of risk, the value of risk management, and has a feel for risk – risk management will not happen.

2 **The risk management process results in action.** Too many risk management processes are about creating paper trails, logs and spreadsheets – and ticking compliance boxes. Unless risk management results in deliberate action it is adding no value.

3 **Risk management is continuous.** Risk management is often pursued on a periodic basis, for example once a month as part of a risk review session. Of course, this is much better than nothing, but the most effective risk management is an ongoing part of daily project management.

4 **The project plan reflects risks.** There are small risks and big risks. All the big risks need to have some sort of mitigating actions. Those actions should be reflected in the project plans (or project *backlog*). The point of the plan is to shape the activity of the project team. If there are risks that need to be managed, this activity needs to include those related to risk management.

5 **The project manager understands the risk profile.** Risks come and go. Events happen which increase or decrease risk. Some of these events are under the control of the project manager and some are not. But in simple terms, at the start of a project, the project has a certain maximum risk profile. At the end of a successful project the risk, or at least the project delivery risk, is zero. Good project managers understand this profile through the life of the project and understand which actions or events change the risk profile as the project progresses. A great test for whether you are in control of risk or not is to ask yourself what are the key events or milestones on the project which align with a decrease in the overall delivery risk – and how does this level of risk change over the projected life of the project. If you know this, then risk management is real (see overleaf).

It is not only the project team who can contribute to effective risk management. A sponsor and stakeholder community who understand that projects are subject to risks and are engaged in the process also helps. Such a sponsor expects to be updated on the risk profile and how it is changing as the project progresses. This sponsor will demand action from the project manager and project team to reduce risk levels. If your sponsor is not like this, they need help and education to see the importance of risk management.

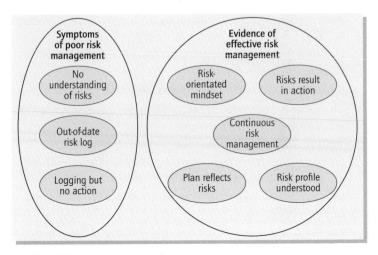

Making risk management real

Project manager's checklist

- Be aware of and alert for the symptoms of poor risk management

- Make risk management an ongoing and active part of the project leading to regular action reflected in the project plan

- Ideally, the sponsor and stakeholder community should engage in and support risk management

The temptations and costs of multi-tasking

What is this about and why is it important?

Multi-tasking is a part of life. We are all used to juggling multiple activities and working on them in parallel. The era of portable smart devices which continuously ping us with calls, text messages, instant messages, emails and updates to social networks seems to have increased the degree of multi-tasking required. Members of project teams are no exception. Their lives are often plagued by multi-tasking.

Team members may work on multiple aspects of the project in parallel, or juggle their involvement in the project with other projects and non-project activities. We seem to take such multi-tasking for granted. We present the people who multi-task most as the objects of veneration. Yet in reality, multi-tasking reduces project team productivity, sometimes significantly. By optimising the levels of multi-tasking in project teams, project managers can improve productivity.

Objectives

- To encourage differentiation between essential multi-tasking and that done by choice
- To reduce the level of multi-tasking to the essential only
- To support project managers in minimising multi-tasking in project teams

Common issues in achieving these objectives

- Social, peer and management pressures to take on more work tasks, combined with an inability or unwillingness to say 'no' or 'yes, but later'
- Lack of understanding of the cost of multi-tasking
- A culture which reveres the heroic juggler

The guide

The ability to multi-task is a necessary skill. None of us lives in an environment in which we can shut ourselves off from the world and only consider one thing at a time. There are essential and unavoidable interruptions in everyone's working lives. Some tasks naturally have pauses in them – for example, a project team ordering equipment faces delays between the order being made and the equipment arriving. It is normal and productive during this waiting period to seek other activities to do. Additionally, we all have a boredom threshold. Some tasks are boring and so we work on them in short bursts until we reach that threshold, then we take a break and move onto something more stimulating for a while. For all these reasons, project team members multi-task.

However, just because multi-tasking is essential does not mean we should seek to exacerbate it. Multi-tasking is usually considerably less efficient than working on tasks in series until they are complete. We should not confuse a frequent necessity with a universal inevitability.

Project managers and project teams should seek to minimise the level of multi-tasking. Some *project management* techniques, specifically some forms of *agile* and approaches like *kanban* have this thinking ingrained into them. Unfortunately, the culture of juggling multiple activities is firmly entrenched in many organisations' ethos, and this carries over into projects.

There are two underlying *assumptions* which need to be challenged:

1 Being 100% busy is the ideal to strive for and leads to the greatest output.

2 The best performers always work on many things at once.

Both of these assumptions are wrong. Whilst it may be counter-intuitive, the busiest are not always the most productive. In a project it is productivity we should measure success by, not hours of exertion. Secondly, whilst we should have sympathy for and perhaps admire the people who have to and can effectively multi-task, we should not seek to emulate them.

One reason for multi-tasking is poor prioritisation. If we do not decide which is the most important task out of all the tasks we can do, then the end result is typically to divide our time across a wide set of activities in parallel. This is a reason why prioritisation is so important (see p. 131).

Consider an example. Four 25-day tasks are to be performed by one person, and each of these tasks produces a valuable deliverable. If the tasks are done in parallel, it seems logical that after 100 days they will all be complete and four deliverables will be available. However, if instead they were done in series, one deliverable would be complete every 25 days. After 25 days one deliverable is ready, after 50 days two and so on until after 100 days all four are ready. It seems that after 100 days the result is the same – but in the interim by working in parallel nothing was available, whilst by working in series there was a growing set of valuable deliverables from 25 days onwards.

In fact, the example shown in the diagram (overleaf) seriously underestimates how bad parallel tasking can be. There is plenty of evidence that shows we lose time every time we switch between tasks. Going back to the example, if the four tasks are done in parallel they will typically take longer than 100 days, often much longer.

This inefficiency increases dramatically when we consider tasks that require several people. If each of the involved individuals are multi-tasking themselves, the inefficiency typically grows exponentially. We have all had to wait weeks to have a one-hour meeting with half a dozen people, or waited for little tasks to be completed which only need a few hours' work but take months to get done.

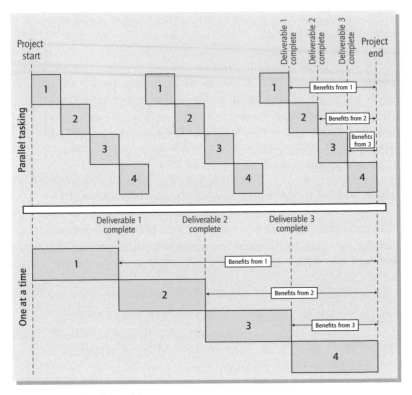

The impact of multi-tasking

The tendency of businesses to set up shared resource pools which projects must use for certain key tasks tends to increase this inefficiency. Shared resource pools go under many names: centres of excellence, expert teams and so on. Such shared resource pools tend to specialise in a functional skill used across many projects, rather than taking accountability for complete project delivery. Many projects contend for the resources in the shared resource pool, and the shared resource pool team members work on many projects in parallel.

Shared resource pools often mistake resource efficiency (having everyone 100% busy) with project efficiency (the best way to deliver the project). They are not the same thing, and can be competing *objectives* (see p. 39). Unfortunately, some teams are even performance managed around utilisation rather than output targets.

If you are a project manager, aim for the best way to deliver the project. If some of your resources come from shared resource pools try to get individuals allocated to the project for 100% of the time you need them – even if this means they are sometimes less than 100% busy. If they time slice between your project and others, the inefficiency will grow and the duration of the project increases significantly.

We should not be naive. Not all resources can be allocated 100% to a project. Not everyone has the luxury of working on one thing at a time. But whenever we or others find ourselves multi-tasking we should challenge the situation and make sure it is essential and we are not doing it simply because we choose to.

Project manager's checklist

- The ability to multi-task is an essential skill for all project managers and project teams

- Multi-tasking is a necessity in some situations, but it should not be extended beyond those situations in which it is essential. As a general principle, minimise multi-tasking

- Try to get resources allocated 100% to the project, even if they will be less than 100% busy all the time

The right and wrong uses of the plan on a page

What is this about and why is it important?

There is a common tendency in business nowadays for project managers to produce a 'plan on a page'. This document is often created as a one-page PowerPoint slide. It provides, at a glance, an overview of the key activities of the project, the overall timescale, and sometimes a very high-level view of the dependency between key activities. This has become such a common tendency that senior managers seem to expect a presentation of a plan in this format. Such a presentation is a standard part of many *sponsor*, *steering committee* and *stakeholder* updates.

Such a plan on a page can be a powerful and useful communication device, but it can also cause problems and *risks* for projects. This section looks at when it is helpful to use a plan on a page and when it is not.

Objectives

- To understand in which situations it is appropriate to use a plan on a page
- To generally gain a better understanding of the various ways in which plans are used
- To use the right type of plan for the right situation

Common issues in achieving these objectives

- Senior managers demanding plans on single pages
- Poor understanding of the different needs and uses of a plan by different audiences
- Poor or lazy *project management* resulting in a lack of detailed planning

The guide

Across my writing and comments on project management, I frequently stress the need for good communications, developing relationships with stakeholders and tailoring communications to the various audiences interested in a project.

One of the challenges for project managers is to communicate complex plans. Showing a detailed *MS Project* plan with several hundred lines to key stakeholders is generally not helpful. Similarly, referring to a complex *backlog*, managed through a tool like *Jira*, in a steering committee meeting is also not particularly useful. In both situations, there is too much detail in such complex plans for senior managers to gain the high-level picture of the project they require.

Senior managers interested in or sponsoring a project are a critical audience to understand plans, but usually only at a relatively shallow level of detail. One good way to explain the project to this group is to produce a plan on a page which gives them a view of the key chunks of work on the project, and usually has a timeline which shows only months or even quarters of time. The plan on a page can be tailored to different audiences to stress the elements of the project they are most interested in.

Unfortunately, I increasingly see project managers using the plan on a page as the only project plan. There is a real difference between the plan on a page as a communication device, and the plan on a page being used as *the* project plan.

As a communication device the plan on a page can be excellent. It can give an overview, understanding and a sense of a project's direction. It is also critical in setting management expectations, and sometimes commitment making. But that is about all. It is a communications and *stakeholder management* tool rather than a project management tool.

You cannot estimate resources, assess the impact of dependencies or work out *critical paths* with a plan on a page. Such a plan does not assist in managing project risk, nor does it provide sufficient detail to assess and control external dependencies. More fundamentally, having only a plan on a page indicates that the project manager and project team have not thought through the project.

Developing a project plan is essential in estimating resources, timelines, risks and so on. But it is not just the output from planning that is important, it is the process itself. Developing a detailed project plan forces the project manager and the project team to think about and understand the project. If you have not developed your own detailed plan, you do not fully understand your project.

Of course, there are sometimes small projects of limited complexity that can fit a fully detailed plan on a page. But using a plan on a page as the only project plan, for an initiative of any complexity, is either laziness or incompetence.

The critical point with any plan is to design it based on what it will be used for. Project plans have multiple uses, which include:

- providing an understanding of the activities involved in a project;
- enabling the project team, sponsor and stakeholders to understand how long a project will take, what resources will be required and how much it will cost to do;
- facilitating communicating and explaining the project to project stakeholders and project team members;
- allowing the project manager to allocate work to different people in the project;
- explaining the project to external audiences impacted by the outcome of the project;
- providing the basis for managing projects to successful completion;
- supporting wider business planning and management commitment making.

There may be a different plan for each of these uses, or ideally the same planning data presented in different ways and to varying levels of detail.

Project manager's checklist

- Project plans have multiple uses and are of interest to different audiences

- Each use and audience may require a different plan, or at least a different presentation of the plan

- The plan on a page can be a useful way to present the project plan to senior audiences

- The plan on a page is not sufficient to manage most projects

- If the only plan is a plan on a page, it indicates insufficient understanding of the project

Audit, assure, control or coach the project?

What is this about and why is it important?

Project management processes have been designed to reduce the *risk* of project failure and increase the likelihood of project success. But nothing is foolproof. Project managers and teams are human and do not always go about things in the right way. Situations are unique and even the best methods can fail when pushed to extreme. Therefore a set of supporting activities have been developed to increase the likelihood of project success.

These activities can be grouped together under the title of *quality management (QM)*. Quality management covers a range of options, including *governance, quality assurance (QA), quality control (QC)*, management or peer reviews, coaching and project audits.

Objectives

- To ensure sufficient quality management is undertaken
- To select the most appropriate quality management approach

Common issues in achieving these objectives

- Insufficient emphasis on quality management
- Performing quality interventions with a tick-box mentality purely to meet compliance requirements or just to provide an audit trail
- Applying a 'one size fits all' quality management approach to all projects

The guide

Why perform quality management?

There is a range of terminology relating to mechanisms for assessing projects and helping them deliver the right things in the right way: governance, quality control, quality assurance, audits, reviews, peer reviews, coaching and so on. Let me bundle all of these into the catch-all title of quality management (QM). In setting up a project there are choices to be made about how to approach QM which affect the cost, timescale and resulting quality of the project.

The starting point for QM should not be to ask what QM is needed, but to understand the QM goals you have. There are three different outcomes from any form of QM intervention in a project:

- to provide confidence to external parties (managers, *stakeholders*, regulators, etc.), that a project is being well run and/or it will achieve its desired outcome;
- to reduce the risk of project failure: this may be achieved by ensuring the right process is being used, or that suitable deliverables or work products are being created (closely related to the first point, but is not the same);
- to improve the skills or capabilities of the project team through feedback, instruction or coaching.

The QM choices

The main QM concepts used in project management originated in manufacturing, but they have been adapted for the needs of projects. The specific way QM is applied in projects varies from sector to sector, for example, quality control in IT and manufacturing projects is quite different, but the underlying concepts are the same.

For complex and larger projects, QM activities require significant planning. This is achieved by quality planning. The result of quality planning is the *quality plan*, a documented set of quality activities, procedures and standards for any project. Personally, I am less interested in quality plans than in the activity of quality planning, and even more fundamentally the mindset that designs the appropriate quality activities into the project.

There are two common elements to QM. A degree of disagreement exists about the precise meanings, but essentially the different types of intervention are:

- quality assurance (QA): activities designed to ensure the project is following the right process;
- quality control (QC): activities designed to ensure the deliverables or work products produced by the project are fit for purpose (which includes, but is not limited to, *testing*).

This can be summarised as ensuring the right approach (QA) and right outcome (QC).

QA and QC are mature disciplines for reducing project risk, but they are not the only ones. In addition, there is a range of reviews that projects can undergo of more or less formality. The classic examples of this are management reviews. Whilst these might often feel formal, they are usually unstructured reviews based on whatever managers feel like asking about. The effectiveness of such reviews is often a function of how much direct experience the reviewing manager has in projects. Such reviews can be sensitive as managers are often seen to be judging the team members' performance rather than helping the project.

Because of this, often it is better for a peer, for example another project manager, to review a project. Such peer reviews can be very powerful in identifying weaknesses and opportunities in a project.

An alternative or complement to reviews is to provide a project team with a coach. Rather than seeking to look for risks, and providing external advice on what to do differently, a coach works with a project team to help them develop their own skills, build on strengths, overcome the problems they face, and to approach projects with the right mindset.

Finding the right balance

There is no one way to apply QM which fits all circumstances, but some general guidance can help in deciding the right balance of audit, assurance, control or reviews:

- Make QM proportionate to the needs of the project. In many organisations larger projects tend to automatically have a greater QM overhead. It is better if QM is proportionate to the risk of the project and capability of the team, rather than just project size. A novice team on a critical, high-risk, small project need more QM support than a highly experienced team on a large, low-risk project.

- Avoid QM being just about ticking boxes. It should be a goal-directed activity and designed to achieve your goals – whether that is greater confidence, reduced risk or improved team capabilities. QM should be part of the project not just an overhead, but it does absorb resources so the aim should be to do enough and only enough QM.

- Optimise the timing of QM interventions. Do not leave everything to a post-implementation review or when a project is going off the rails. These are important learning opportunities but experience shows that earlier interventions are better. They will identify and fix problems sooner, reducing the cost and impact of that fix. A problem fixed early in a project's life costs a small fraction of a problem fixed late. However, not everything can be identified at the start and QM interventions should be regular throughout the project's life.

- Minimise specially produced QM review artefacts. Ideally, any QM reviews should be of standard project work products. If the right project artefacts for reviews are hard to produce, this is a sign of a poorly run project or badly designed QM approach. Occasionally, QM seems to need specific artefacts for quality reviews – but this should be avoided as the aim is to review the project, not the QM artefacts.

If this is not done you risk creating 'shadow projects'. This happens when there is a hidden un-reviewed project doing the actual work and a visible parallel project creating unrelated artefacts for compliance checking or box ticking.

- Try to develop a positive attitude to QM activities. Ideally, the project team sees reviews as an opportunity to get better, not as criticism. People performing reviews should approach them as ways to reduce project risk, not a mechanism to catch people out or do performance management. As a reviewer, if you mingle project reviews with performance management, you risk having key information hidden from you.

- Apply a range of interventions with different styles. QA and QC both add value – but they identify different issues and problems. Coaching and auditing can both be helpful. If you want the team to learn then emphasise coaching, if you need to prove external compliance perform audits.

- Balance internal and external reviewers. Ideally, you want a self-improving, self-correcting project team. But some level of external reviews remains important. You want to avoid the 'marking your own homework' scenario. Plus external reviewers often provide fresh insights. Mingling reviewing with coaching is difficult, and it is usually better to separate coaching from reviewing roles. Finally, whilst an experienced peer project manager can add value by reviewing the project management approach, for QC activities you generally need content expertise in the deliverables of the project.

Project manager's checklist

- QM is an important part of a well-run project – reducing project risk, and providing confidence to stakeholders and learning opportunities to project team members

- The most appropriate form of QM depends on the nature and context of the project

- QM should be timely and proportionate to the project risk and capability of the project team
- QM should be an integral part of the project and not an overhead or a box-ticking exercise

The project environment

In the first five parts we looked at projects largely from the perspective of project teams, project managers and sponsors. But projects do not exist in isolation. They operate within an organisation and as a part of a society. The organisation and society shape the needs, pressures, opportunities and risks of a project. Successful projects work well within their specific environment.

The first section of this part looks at one of the most important external impacts on a project: prioritisation. Most organisations have more to do than they have resources to deal with. The effective approach to this is prioritisation – and therefore it is critical how a project is prioritised relative to other activities. The next section looks at how to create a culture of delivery. The simple truth is that some organisations have this culture and deliver projects well, some do not. What are the differentiating factors? The third section looks at the myth that projects can fully predict the future. What are the implications of this and how should you deal with it? Finally, we will look at the wider issue of dealing with problems which are external to a project, but which impact upon it.

Prioritisation

What is this about and why is it important?

Prioritisation is crucial for effective delivery. From a project perspective there are two levels of prioritisation: the priority the project is given relative to other projects in the organisation, and the prioritisation of activities within the project relative to other possible activities. Conceptually, the process for prioritisation is the same at both levels, but the level of formality, complexity and responsibilities vary. This section applies to both: the project and activity levels.

We prioritise because we have insufficient resource to do everything we might. Without co-ordinated priorities, a team will be inefficient – often, extremely inefficient. Even if you have enough resources within a project, prioritisation is still needed. Some tasks bring more benefit than others, and should be done first.

Prioritisation is a form of decision making. Prioritisation decisions have to take account of contending business needs. For example, balancing doing today's work, keeping *stakeholders* happy, fixing short-term problems or achieving the longer-term visions. In prioritising, you seek to allocate your limited resources to the most important needs.

Objectives

- To provide clarity on what is important and what is not, and in which order activities should be completed
- To ensure the most important tasks are completed first
- To be able to identify the symptoms of poor prioritisation

- Prioritisation is not regarded as important, and so is not done
- Prioritisation is perceived as too hard to do, especially in complex and volatile environments
- Prioritisation is often poorly implemented

The guide

There is no painless way to prioritise. It takes effort, and an understanding of options and resource constraints. Although prioritisation requires analysis, it is above all an exercise in decision making. Even when the choice is obvious, it may mean an uncomfortable decision resulting in some dissatisfied stakeholders.

Prioritisation criteria

The logic of prioritisation is straightforward. List the possible projects (activities). Work out how important each project (activity) is. Then order the most important first and least important last. But, success in prioritisation is not starting the most important task first. It is *finishing* the most important one first.

Putting this into practice can be hard. We often do not know what is most important, or what the definition of importance is. Prioritisation begins by understanding prioritisation criteria. Understanding what is important can be of greater consequence than actually prioritising. If you understand what is important and what is not, your decision making will be easy and fast. If you do not know this, then it will always be difficult.

Typical criteria to judge importance of projects are financial measures, alignment with strategic goals or meeting some specific stakeholder objective. Avoid using too few or too many criteria on which you judge the importance of projects. Use too many criteria and you will get bogged down in analysis. Too few criteria usually results in overly simplistic project choices. To prioritise activities within a project, an intuitive feel for prioritisation is normally sufficient.

Setting priorities

With a project, decide how prescriptive you need to be in setting priorities. At one extreme is direction setting. Here you give enough information for team members to decide their own priorities. For a small and mature project team this is usually enough. At the other extreme, you may need to perform a prescriptive ranking of all activities. In certain high-pressure situations, and for less-experienced project teams, this may be required.

Ideally, team members develop their abilities to make choices about importance based on broad guidance. However, if you need to be prescriptive, be prescriptive! Do not roughly bundle things into high, medium or low categories. Make clear what is top priority, what is bottom priority and what must be stopped. Often defining what needs to stop is a quick way to a significantly more efficient team. Another advantage of clear prioritisation is that it minimises the need to multi-task which is inherently inefficient (see p. 113).

Regularly revisit prioritisations, but do not change priorities all the time or nothing will get done. Revisit priorities at least once a month and amend according to needs. The duration for which priorities are set depends on the context and the *project management* style you are using. *Agile* teams revisit priorities after every *sprint. Waterfall* teams may do so less often – but it is still worth doing regularly.

It is not the absolute importance of tasks that matters, but the relative importance between the different components of the team's workload. From time to time there will be some important tasks that cannot be done because you have even more important things to do.

Keep the prioritisation process simple. Remember that getting things done is more important than the activity of prioritising.

Prioritisation should be rapid and straightforward. At first it will be hard, but regular practice will make it brisk and efficient. Do not be afraid of making a prioritisation decision. If you get it wrong – you can easily change it.

Ensure it is working

Test the effectiveness of your prioritisation. Check how clear team members are and how consistent their activities are with agreed priorities. Observe the choices being made and activities being stopped. Prioritisation must result in a choice being made between alternatives. If you spend time prioritising and decide that everything is important, effectively you have made no decision.

Here are some common situations which exemplify poor prioritisation:

- **There is no prioritisation:** managers often struggle with prioritisation. In some organisations there is no attempt to prioritise. Arguments like 'we don't need to prioritise', 'it's too complex' or 'it changes all the time' are made. The form of prioritisation rightly varies, but all organisations and project teams need to prioritise.

- **No-one knows what work is ongoing:** to prioritise you must have an understanding of what the possible and actual work is. Therefore if you do not have this picture, even a very high-level perspective, it is unlikely that any prioritisation is taking place.

- **Priorities are not understood:** it is essential to communicate priorities. Priorities are crucial information to communicate across teams. There is no point going through the effort of prioritising unless everyone is told what the resultant decisions are. As part of the communication of priorities it is important to stress what is high priority, what is low priority and what must stop.

- **Everything is high priority, nothing stops:** a prioritisation process is being undertaken, but it is not effective. The classic example is when a project *portfolio* is prioritised. Projects are prioritised on a scale of 1 to 3. At the end of the prioritisation 95% of the projects are given priority 1. This is not prioritisation: it is weak thinking and failure to make decisions. If prioritisation results in all activities having a high priority, then it is not a useful process. Effective prioritisation results in clear decisions *not* to undertake some activities and in a relatively small selection of high-priority activities to progress.

- **Personal priorities rule:** an absence of explicit prioritisation does not lead to a total lack of prioritisation. In the end, team members have only so many hours in the day and if no prioritisation is indicated, they will prioritise themselves. There is nothing intrinsically wrong with delegating prioritisation decisions, but there are two *risks*. Firstly, unless team members have a well-understood and shared vision of direction, prioritisation decisions taken by different team members will be inconsistent. Secondly, progress will be delayed and resources inefficiently allocated because of the lack of synchronisation between different individuals.

- **Conformity with priorities is poor:** individuals can be surprisingly resistant to priorities they do not like or do not agree with. Project teams can be especially vigorous in ignoring priorities and forcing progress on a project in spite of priorities, rather than in accordance with them.

Project manager's checklist

- Prioritisation starts by understanding what is important

- Do not get overly analytical – prioritisation is a tool, not a result in itself

- Make prioritisation decisions quickly. If they turn out to be wrong revisit and amend

- Monitor and check for compliance to priorities

- Regularly update – but not so frequently that no work gets done

The culture of delivery

What is this about and why is it important?

Project teams do not deliver alone, but as part of larger organisations. Typically, only a small part of the organisation is involved in any one project. However, delivery success is impacted significantly by the culture of this larger organisation.

Many have experienced easier delivery in some organisations compared to others. Some organisations have cultures which encourage delivery, whilst others have cultures which obstruct delivery.

Individual project teams can typically do very little to alter an organisation's culture. But by understanding those characteristics which help delivery and those which hinder it, project teams can take mitigating actions.

Project *sponsors* and executives can take steps to alter a culture, over time. This is worth doing. The cost, time and *risk* of delivering a project in organisations with a supportive culture is less than the cost, time and risk of delivery of the same project in an obstructing organisation.

Objectives

- To understand aspects of organisational culture which help delivery
- To support project planning to take account of the cultural environment
- To help sponsors, *stakeholders* and executives develop a culture of delivery

Culture is ignored, taken for granted or assumed to be unchangeable – the mentality of 'it's just the way we are'

The guide

Culture is a powerful force. There are multiple cultures in any organisation. There are ethnic and national cultures, organisational, departmental and group cultures, and as a project progresses there will be a project team culture. The project manager should account for the culture in the way a project is planned and run.

Let us look at several key cultural attributes which can aid or impede delivery.

Ownership

In the organisational culture which facilitates delivery, people take ownership for actions and tasks.

A good way to understand organisational culture is to observe meetings. Are actions raised and do people naturally tend to stand up and take ownership of these actions? If no-one steps forward and everyone has to be prodded into taking responsibility, then your task as a project manager will be more difficult.

A more subtle version of this problem is when ownership is allocated, but it is allocated to departments and not individuals. In the end, it is not departments that deliver work on projects. It is individual people.

What can you do if you find yourself working in an environment in which ownership and accountability are not easily accepted? You need to be very robust in your planning phase in making sure every task has a named owner. Do not get fobbed off by abstract entities like the names of teams.

Action orientated

In the organisational culture which facilitates delivery, people take accountability for actions; therefore they execute those actions with limited follow-up and reminders.

Unfortunately, this is far from being universally true. In some organisations getting anything done requires constant chasing. Worse there are organisations in which people appear to accept responsibility to deliver something when they are in meetings, but afterwards nothing happens. Some of the most frustrating businesses I have worked in have this feature. Actions are agreed, everyone smiles and says they accept the actions. Then nothing happens.

What can you do if you work in this sort of business? The answer is a relentless focus on progress chasing and continuous reminding of delivery accountabilities and timescales. Waiting for the periodic update meetings is not enough. People in these organisations need ongoing chasing.

Outcome focused

Being action orientated is a great start for a project, but it is not enough. Everyone has heard of the situation of busy fools: people who pride themselves on being busy, but achieve nothing. Often, less-busy people achieve more, simply because what they achieve is valuable or useful.

This is particularly important in projects. Sometimes the focus on completing activities on the plan gets in the way of checking whether the desired outcomes and business benefits are being achieved – or at least progressed towards.

What can you do if you work in an environment which is not outcome focused? Make sure everyone in the project knows *why* the project is being undertaken and what the business case is. Regularly challenge team members, and encourage them to challenge as well, with the question: 'How is what you are doing contributing to achieving our desired outcome?' Review not just activity progress, but progress towards outcomes.

Respecting others' goals

In the organisational culture which facilitates delivery, people respect others' goals. Of course, no organisation has one set of universal goals. There are always conflicts of priorities and *objectives*. But in effective organisations such clashes are accepted as a normal part of business, which need to be calmly resolved.

Unfortunately, this is rarely the case. The culture of performance management seems to encourage staff to avoid helping anyone who is doing something which does not contribute to their own goals. Where conflict arises, battles ensue. Classic things include people playing political games and sending out angry emails with unnecessarily long lists of recipients on the CC line. This is never productive.

What can you do if you work in this type of culture? Before the project kicks off try and ensure everyone who needs to contribute to the project has aligned, or at least not contradictory, goals. If you can, get delivery of the project included in the team's performance objectives. Try to ensure the project has a senior sponsor, who is prepared to intervene regularly. And accept that resolving, or working around, political battles takes time!

Consistency of objectives

In the organisational culture which facilitates delivery there is a consistency of focus, not a daily churn of objectives and priorities. Priorities and strategies may evolve, but it is understood that delivery takes time and constant changes of strategic direction are not helpful.

There are many businesses in which this is not true. In some of them changes of focus cannot be avoided. Some businesses work in very dynamic markets and it is essential to respond to market pressures regularly. But this is not the case for all organisations. The reality is that constant alteration of goals and priorities is usually a result of poor strategic thinking.

What can you do if you work in this kind of business? Only deliver a project relative to the priority it is given. If priorities change then this is a change to the project's conditions. Plans may need to be altered as a response to this. It is not a project manager's role to deliver in spite of priorities, but to deliver taking account of the priority a project is given (see p. 131). But keep sponsors informed, as they need to know the impact. It is the sponsors' and other stakeholders' job to keep the project as a high priority.

Supportive of change

Projects result in change. The change may be simple and minor or can be complex and profound. Some organisations are responsive to change. They are willing to challenge the status quo. Staff and management are open minded, and processes and systems are flexible. Change may be questioned, but in a constructive way.

Of course, this is not always true. Many organisations are inflexible in terms of processes, systems or attitudes. Today's ways are thought best, turf is protected, and any attempt to improve on the status quo is regarded with suspicion, as a threat or an insult to people's past efforts.

What can you do if you work in this kind of business? Plan, prepare and have adequate resource for implementation. Take the human side of change seriously and invest properly in *change management* (see p. 160).

Project knowledgeable sponsors and stakeholders

The best sponsors and stakeholders know how projects work and understand what helps to get outcomes achieved. They do not need to be *project management* experts, but they understand that projects need adequate resources, thrive when objectives are stable, are helped by quick decision making and flourish when the organisation is stable (see p. 223).

Some sponsors, *steering committee* members and stakeholders act in ways which are detrimental to project success. Decisions are made slowly, resources are provided grudgingly and requirements and objectives keep changing. Sometimes this is unavoidable because of the situation an organisation is in, but often it is simply ignorance or inexperience in leading projects.

What can you do in this type of culture? Try to educate the sponsor and other key stakeholders as the project progresses. Explain their roles and how they can help the project (see pp. 20 and 66). Sensitively manage their involvement in the project as for any other resource. But be realistic in your project planning about the expected nature of stakeholder engagement and how this will impact the progress.

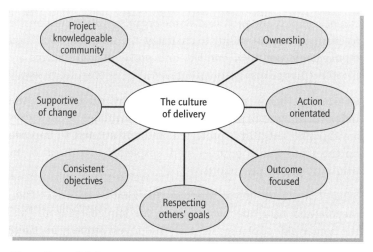

The culture of delivery

Project manager's checklist

- ▓ Organisational culture has a significant impact on the success, costs and timescale that projects take

- ▓ Project teams cannot directly alter culture, but must plan to operate effectively within it

- ▓ Project sponsors, senior stakeholders and executives should work to develop cultures which support delivery

The limits to planning and prediction

What is this about and why is it important?

The culture of business values detailed predictions above broad-brush estimates, and likes predictions that enable dependable commitment making. Businesses praise project managers whose results or actuals match their predictions. Project managers who do not predict accurately are seen as poor project managers.

Project managers build plans by determining the activities needed to meet project outcomes. Then they estimate the durations and ordering of the activities, and the resources required. Plans are based on analysis, experience, models, *assumptions* and, if we are honest, guesses.

Earlier we looked at developing a plan (see p. 39). In this section, I will discuss some pitfalls to avoid in planning, and why striving for the most accurately predicted future is not always best.

Objectives

- To help project managers in making the best plans for their projects
- To understand the boundaries of predictability

Common issues in achieving these objectives

Management culture which insists on certainty, and which makes admitting to limits of predictability seem like failure

The guide

The most obvious problem with planning is that there is always too little information to make perfectly accurate predictions. On top of this, the world changes and so the conditions at the time of the prediction are not the same as at the time of the result. We have limited foresight. Good planning therefore makes *risks* and assumptions explicit. More sophisticated plans even include sensitivity analysis around the risks.

In addition to limited foresight, there are other problems with planning which derive from the behaviour of managers in many organisations.

Planning limitations

Project planning is not a science whose pronouncements have the validity of laws of nature. At best, plans are based on a series of reasonably consistent empirical viewpoints derived from limited samples of data. There are exceptions, but usually rules applied are rules of thumb. Planning forecasts often concern the behaviour of people, and behaviour is notoriously difficult to predict. There is nothing wrong with this as long as the limitation of planning is borne in mind.

There is no reliable algorithm or rules for decomposing project *objectives* into a series of tasks to achieve each objective. It has to be done by analysis, and such analysis is error prone.

Some projects are unique. If you have never done something before, your confidence should be moderate at best in determining how long it will take and therefore what resources it requires.

Other projects seem similar to previous initiatives, yet vary in the conditions and context in which they operate. Assuming a task will take as long and use the same resources as previous projects is risky. Conditions are never exactly the same. It is not even clear what makes conditions sufficiently similar for an activity to be completely predictable.

Behaviour

Another issue is management behaviour. There are three common challenges to the development of good project plans:

- **The planning game:** project managers know that understandings are incomplete and hence build in safety factors into predictions. Their managers expect this, and it results in the planning game: project managers ask for as much as they can, and their line managers challenge them and try to reduce requests as much as possible. Neither side really knows what is required – but the assumption is that if the project manager is challenged enough, the resulting compromise will be right.

- **Attitudes to contingency:** well-designed plans take account of the risk in prediction making by including contingency in the plan. Mature organisations accept this. Unfortunately, many managers see contingency as something to be squeezed or removed. It is considered as 'fat' in the plan to be squeezed out.

- **Making the outcome fit the predictions:** the unspoken primary aim of the project in some situations is to ensure actuals match predictions. Achieving the desired project outcomes is a secondary aim. Project work is managed to match predictions to the actuals, sometimes to the detriment of project outcomes.

Better information about the future?

Even if the planning is flawed, surely what plans try to achieve is right? If we continue to collect evidence and build better planning models will this not solve the problem? It will help, but it will not solve the underlying problem. The problem is not just the way the standard planning model achieves its objective but that the objective of having perfect predictability is flawed.

Perfect predictability is a myth, an unobtainable goal. Project managers should be aiming for the best result, not the most predictable. You do not just want better planning algorithms and even more data. You want a more realistic understanding of what is and what is not plannable – and ways of dealing with this reality.

What is plannable comes down to how far into the future you can predict with any reliability:

▦ **The horizon of confidence:** that is how far into the future you can predict with confidence. This depends on context. In many cases this is quite short. It may be a few days, weeks or at best months. Within this horizon it is worth making detailed plans.

▦ **The horizon of foresight:** you can make useful forecasts further into the future. You may be less confident of the accuracy, but they can be used to communicate intentions and facilitate preparation. However, making plans beyond the horizon of confidence in any detail is wasted effort. High-level plans and roadmaps are all that is worth doing.

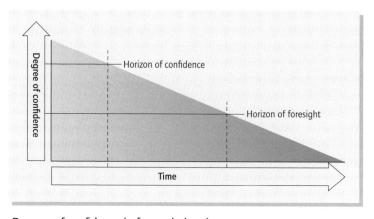

Degrees of confidence in forward planning

There are many tools and techniques to improve plans. Classic *project management* tools such as *assumption management, risk management* and contingency planning help. Also there are ways to improve *work breakdown structure* development and estimations – and these are continuously being enhanced.

You should keep up to date. Do not rely on the planning techniques and estimation principles you used years ago. Techniques improve and experience expands the ability to predict, but this cannot remove the fundamental challenge of the horizon of confidence.

Better approaches accept that you cannot predict accurately and apply project techniques which focus on making near-term commitments, leaving flexibility for the future. The technique for traditional projects is *progressive elaboration* – plans are progressively detailed as time passes. Another is *agile*, which makes commitments for the short term and leaves the longer run more flexible.

But – plan!

The conclusion from this may seem to be: why bother to make predictions? There are good reasons why you should bother.

The first is that planning and budgeting are part of the ritual of business. Every organisation has its own rituals and customs, and if you want to be part of it you need to conform. If you do not play along, your project will not get off the ground. As much as anything, planning processes are political processes. You will be judged not simply by your results, but how well you act the expected role of a project manager in performing these activities.

Secondly, flawed is not the same as being of no use. Good plans, used appropriately, are powerful. Although it may be rare, there are some situations in which you understand the conditions well, and your level of accuracy in a long-term forecast will be high. But even when not, forecasts and plans are useful, as long as:

- you use them as a project management tool, not the oracle of truth;
- you understand the degree of accuracy and sensitivities in plans as well as your horizons of confidence;
- you are aware of and manage the risks and assumptions made in plans;

- you put in realistic levels of contingency.

Finally, whilst I am sceptical about how far forward you can accurately plan, this should never be used as an excuse for not planning. Planning is an essential project management tool. It just needs to be done in the right way, accepting the limits of predictability.

Project manager's checklist

- There are limits to your ability to plan and make predictions

- A project manager's primary objective is to achieve project outcomes; making actuals match predictions should be secondary

- There are many approaches to better planning, and project managers should use these and regularly update their knowledge

- But even the best tools do not change the fact that there is a limit to how far you can predict with accuracy

Dealing with external problems

What is this about and why is it important?

Projects have a limited *scope*. You could argue that they must have a limited scope, or else they might never end. The scope of a project is not a given, but is a choice made in designing the project. Rarely, in defining the scope, is it possible to isolate the project completely from the effects of outside events.

External events can impact any project. Projects typically have dependencies on activities outside of the project manager's direct control, and generally operate in environments which cannot be fully managed by the project team.

Sometimes external events contribute to the smooth running of a project. In other situations external factors cause problems for a project: dependencies are late and events occur to the detriment of the project. Most *project management* practices, processes and tools support managing the activities within a project's scope. The challenge is: how should the project team deal with external problems?

External events are the source of a large proportion of the *risks* on most projects. A way of predicting and responding to external problems can result in these risks being avoided, or at least being reduced.

It might be thought that the whole point of defining the project's scope is to set a hard boundary beyond which the project team need not venture. But a good project team cannot shrug their shoulders and ignore problems outside of their control if the result is a failing project. The scope defines a boundary, but it is a permeable one.

Objective

■ To reduce the risk of external events or actions which cause detrimental effects to a project

→ Tendency for project teams to focus on obvious and close proximity issues

→ Attitude of 'if it's out of scope, it's not my problem'

→ Poor *assumption management*

The guide

The options for external problems

Earlier we looked at defining scope (see p. 26). Scope defines what is 'in' and 'out' of the project. Anything not 'in' is external. In this section, I want to describe options for dealing with external problems.

In the simplest terms, there are four options for dealing with external problems:

1 to ignore external events and the risk of problems they might pose for a project, and live with the consequences during the project, whatever they are;

2 to take full ownership for resolving external problems (effectively an enlargement of the project's scope);

3 to cut external dependencies and remove the ability of external events to influence a project;

4 to influence external parties to take ownership for external problems and to resolve them in a way that meets the needs of the project.

Each of these options is the right solution in some situations.

Some external problems should be ignored as they are of a low probability and outside the project team's ability to influence.

For example, if the office a project team is working in burns down this will stop the project, but in most situations this is highly unlikely and is something no individual project manager can predict or influence. The only sensible response in this situation is to forget about the issue, and respond if and when the unlikely event occurs. This cannot be the answer to all external problems, as it results in projects suffering from issues that can be effectively and efficiently avoided or resolved.

Other external problems are best dealt with by the project team extending the project's scope and dealing with the problem themselves. For example, an IT project developing new software may wish to include purchasing and installing the necessary hardware required to implement the software. But this should not be undertaken unless the project team has the resources and capability to resolve the issue and the team is best placed to resolve it. On many occasions, the team is incapable of resolving the problem and still delivering the project. Or the team may be able to resolve the problem, but should leave it to an external team who are better placed or skilled to resolve it.

There are some situations in which the risk of impact on a project from external events can be reduced or even removed completely. A simple example is when someone funding a project has to reduce the project's budget. One solution is to cut the dependency on this funding by finding alternative financial sources. Contingency plans and creative thinking can reduce many external dependencies – but unfortunately not all.

Finally, often the best approach is to influence or persuade other parties to take proper ownership for the delivery of external dependencies and the resolution of external problems, and to solve them in a way that suits your project's needs. Being able to persuade others to do this, or persuade your *stakeholders* to influence or direct others to do this, is an important project management skill. Unfortunately, this does not always work. The history of project management is littered with projects which failed due to external problems that no-one took ownership of.

An approach to managing external problems

Each of the four options described above helps to resolve some external issues, but none of them is a foolproof solution to all external problems. A project manager has to balance these options, and must actively manage external dependencies and risks, and the impact of external issues when they occur.

A good approach is to:

1 Identify all external dependencies and risks early in the project's *lifecycle*, ideally during the planning and budgeting phase.

2 Actively manage these as part of the project's *risk management* process, choosing the most appropriate of the above four options for each risk.

3 Manage *assumptions* relating to external dependencies. External dependencies are often 'resolved' by logging assumptions. Do not just log such assumptions at the start of the project and then forget them. Assumptions must be actively monitored, and if they turn out to be wrong, or have a significant probability of being wrong, should be dealt with.

4 Manage the expectations of the *sponsor, steering committee* and other key stakeholders regarding external risks and the limits of your capability to resolve them if realised.

5 Try to use your influence and persuasion to make sure the appropriate owners of external dependencies understand the impact on your project and are treating you as an important customer. Use your sponsor and steering committee members to help in this. A productive use of a steering committee is to help in ensuring the project is running in a supportive environment in which external dependencies are well managed by appropriate owners.

6 Monitor key external events, but do not try to manage all of them. Unless you choose to bring them in scope, they are not the project manager's to manage. But they must be

monitored for progress towards resolving, and any changes in status tracked in line with other project risks.

7 Keep doing steps 2–6. If something does go wrong respond, and implement your contingency plans!

Project manager's checklist

■ External dependencies and events are a major source of risks for projects

■ Project managers can respond by: ignoring external dependencies, bringing them in scope to resolve, cutting the dependency or getting someone external to the project to take ownership

■ None of these solutions will work for all external issues. It is best to apply a combination of these responses combined with active risk management

Integrated project management

Project management is a wide-ranging discipline. Depending on the context, history and culture of a project team the approach to delivering projects varies considerably. Anyone who has worked on both software and infrastructure projects soon sees this difference. One important aspect of this is how project management integrates with surrounding disciplines. An ability to integrate project management effectively with other management disciplines is a real factor in project success.

The first section of this part looks at project management generally. What are its strengths and limitations, and therefore what supporting disciplines should project teams bring in and utilise. The second section discusses one particularly grey area: the relationship and boundaries between project and change managers. The third section explores the area which is often treated with less importance than it should, the link from project management to benefits realisation. The final section looks at what project management can learn from two of the most successful management developments over the past few decades: lean and six sigma.

The strengths and limits of project management

What is this about and why is it important?

This book is concerned with the application of *project management* to achieve the outcomes organisations require. But what is the right area of application? For project management to be effective you must apply the right form of project management in the right situations, in the right way to the right sorts of problems. You must understand the strengths and weaknesses of project management.

Additionally, there are situations in which project team members need to explain project management to *stakeholders*. To do this successfully it is useful to be clear about the strengths, weaknesses and limits to project management.

Objectives

- To understand the advantages, disadvantages and limitations of project management
- To support decisions concerning when and how to apply project management
- To help explain the strengths and weaknesses of project management to interested parties

Common issues in achieving these objectives

Tendency not to question approaches or seek to understand *why* things are done in certain ways

The guide

The advantages of project management

Projects are undertaken to achieve some desired outcomes or *objectives*. But why use project management as opposed to any other management approach? The advantages of applying project management vary from project to project, but we can identify generic advantages that are attained when project management is properly applied to appropriate situations. The advantages described here are relative to the situation in which people muddle through to achieve desired outcomes without project management.

- **Complexity and *risk* are managed:** project management provides a way of managing the complexity of activities required to achieve certain outcomes, and provides the tools to control the associated risks. Without this, many outcomes cannot be achieved.

- **Efficient resource usage:** both people and money are used efficiently in a well-defined and run project.

- **Reduced cost and timescale:** a well-designed project provides an efficient way to achieve the end result, combined with improved quality of outcomes.

- **Commitment making:** project plans enable organisations to make commitments internally, to *stakeholders* and shareholders, as well as to customers and suppliers. This is essential in many organisations.

- **Provides confidence:** by setting expectations and delivering against them, projects provide confidence to clients and stakeholders. This is the basis of a healthy and productive relationship with stakeholders. It can also provide the impression of professionalism which is important in many businesses.

- **Good environment for teams and team work:** the structure project management provides is the basis for productive, motivated and happy project team members.

The disadvantages of project management

The primary disadvantage of project management is captured in the adage 'nothing comes for free'. Project management creates an overhead in terms of additional activities in the work needed to achieve an outcome. It introduces roles that do not directly create value-adding work products but only facilitate the process of their creation: a project manager is one such role. However, when project management is properly applied this overhead is amply recouped by the efficiencies gained in resource usage, time and quality of outcomes.

Other disadvantages come less from project management, than from the negative behaviour of some project managers and project team members. This counter-productive behaviour is reinforced by simplistic interpretations of project management, poor judgement and by some organisational cultures. Typical examples of such unhelpful behaviour include:

- **Rigid and inflexible work styles:** resulting in the blocking of creativity.

- **Putting project management compliance before outcomes:** greater emphasis on the correct application of processes, practices and methodologies than the achievement of the business outcomes. For example, box ticking, obsession with creating perfect rather than good enough project documentation, etc.

- **Obsessive focus on achieving the plan:** rather than trying to achieve the outcome in the most efficient and effective way. A plan should be an evolving guide, not treated as the one source of the truth. Obsession with keeping to the plan tends to occur in organisations in which hitting targets and ensuring *actuals* equal plan are important and in which performance management and rewards encourage meeting predictions (see p. 142).

- **Lack of alignment with the organisation:** projects work outside normal operations. This risks project staff having insufficient understanding of operational reality.

Additionally, project managers tend to push for stable objectives, whilst real business needs change.

The limits to project management

Project management provides an effective way to deliver some activities, but not all. Examples of situations in which project management is less successful are when:

- free form and unconstrained thinking are required, for example, creative generation of ideas;
- performing operational tasks;
- delivering ongoing maintenance.

But there are no hard and fast boundaries. Some maintenance tasks are big and complex and need to be projects. Flow management techniques like *kanban* are great for managing workloads of large numbers of activities, such as in software application maintenance. Such techniques blur the boundary between project management and maintenance and operational tasks. There are some tasks which are definitely operational, others which are definitely projects, but there is a grey area in between.

Systemic issues

Projects often need to resolve issues. A key skill of project teams is the ability to identify and resolve impediments to progress. But sometimes the issues which impact a project are too big, complex or outside the boundaries of a project or even a series of projects to resolve. Such *systemic issues* exist because of the environment in which projects operate.

Even the best project management methodology cannot resolve all systemic issues. Examples include:

- untimely or unresponsive management decision making;
- poor prioritisation;

- inefficient resource management policies and organisational design;
- unskilled or low-capability project team members;
- insufficient resources;
- a culture which does not support projects;
- poor project selection or objective setting, especially when unconnected to real business needs;
- unreasonable and unmanageable stakeholder expectations.

In each case project management helps by giving the project manager the tools and information to assist other people to see the nature and impact of these problems. But project management can only help to resolve them – it cannot fix them completely. The related disciplines of *programme* and *portfolio management* can be more helpful in some of these areas, but again only to a certain extent. However, wider management actions and decisions can remove these systemic issues if the choice is made to do so. (Designing the environment for projects is discussed on pp. 136 and 249.)

The right approach

Even when you are involved in delivering something that should be a project, it does not mean that any one specific project management technique should be used. All project management techniques have a range of application.

Think about ends and means. The desired project outcome is the end, and in the longer run that is all that matters. The means by which you achieved the end, as long as they are efficient and effective (legal and ethical!), are irrelevant. Project management processes, practices, tools and techniques are means. The only reason to use them is because they help to achieve the ends. If they do not work, or are not helping to achieve the ends effectively and efficiently, drop them and use something better.

Project challenges vary, but so do the types of project management. For example, there are *agile, iterative* and *waterfall* techniques. The advocates of each tend to present them as the one true way of running all projects. In truth, they each have their place. A rather simple set of criteria for choosing a particular approach could be:

- for situations which are volatile and exhibit ongoing change – agile;
- when customers do not know what they want and it cannot be determined by analysis – iterative;
- where there is a degree of stability and when long-term commitment making is required – waterfall.

Each of these statements may be overly simplistic, contentious and the subject of thousands of discussions, articles and books. The underlying point is straightforward: use the most appropriate method for your conditions, and as conditions vary, vary your approach.

Project manager's checklist

- There are advantages and disadvantages of project management. Most of the disadvantages relate to how it is applied rather than the approach itself
- Project management generally, and each project management approach individually, has areas of application in which it is most effective
- Projects suffer from a range of systemic issues which project management alone cannot resolve

Bridging the divide: project and change managers

What is this about and why is it important?

Project management and *change management* are natural partners. Many projects result in change, many changes require a project to deliver the components of that change. Unfortunately, project and change managers often act as isolated communities, each separately trying to deliver innovation and enhancements.

Many members of these communities know of, but remain relatively uninformed about, the other. In a business context there are significant gains to be achieved by bringing these communities together.

Objective

■ To encourage project and change managers to work together synergistically

Common issues in achieving this objective

Lack of mutual understanding and lack of common vocabulary

Tendency for each community to try and own the whole of change delivery

The guide

Ask a group of project managers about change, and the typical response is, 'We know about change – all projects deliver change'. Ask a group of change managers about project management and the typical response is, 'Well project management is OK as far as it goes, but change is not something that can be shaped into a task list and managed as a deliverable'.

Project management communities talk as if they own change management. Some project managers think they have a good understanding of change and change management. But if you question them about the change tools and techniques they know and use, this understanding is usually shallow. Change management communities tend to downplay or even completely ignore project management. Pick up a best-selling change management book and try to find the word 'project' – or a project management book and see how much is really about change. There are exceptions, but in general this picture is accurate.

There are dual-skilled individuals around, but they are relatively few and far between. Change managers who think in terms of projects tend to design high-level plans which show a visionary pathway forward without worrying too much about adherence to the plan. Project managers who know about change tend to use only approaches that are suited to or can be built into a *work breakdown structure*.

How did it come about?

Project management has a long history. It was formally defined in the mega projects of the first half of the twentieth century and grew from the experience of engineers struggling to get complex tasks completed. It has since become increasingly formalised. Various associations have developed *bodies of knowledge*, and academics have got in on the act studying and analysing project management. Although it is a broad discipline, its origins in engineering are obvious.

Change management has as long a history, but its existence as a specific discipline originated in the writings of academics like Kurt Lewin in the middle of the twentieth century. Lewin was a psychologist – the father of social psychology – but his writings are rarely read now by change managers. However, change management owes a lot to early pioneers like Lewin. Even if we now have different tools and models, dig deeper and you soon feel the origins in analysing individual and group behaviour.

Project and change management have disconnected origins, different cultures of practitioners and separate languages of debate. Having started apart, they tend to stay distinct. Those interested in one discipline tend to have a limited awareness and education in the other. Project managers focus on deliverables, change practitioners on people and teams. This is a shame, for they share goals – delivering lasting improvements. Goals that require both creating deliverables and working with people and teams to adopt them.

What can we do about it?

Project managers should reach out to understand change management more, but we should also understand the limitation of the role in any situation and decide quite how much change management is our responsibility.

The fundamental question for a project manager is to determine whether you are responsible for creating deliverables or delivering an outcome. By deliverable I mean something like an IT system, new building or process design. By outcome I mean achieving the lasting change that is required to achieve a business case. If it is deliverables, then the subsequent question is who owns the outcome? If it is clearly not you, you can stick to the nuts and bolts of creating deliverables. If you are responsible for an outcome, and what is wanted is a long-term sustained outcome, then you better know something about change management. Additionally, if you really want to excel in your career then creating deliverables is not enough – it is outcomes that deliver value in business. A track record in delivering positive outcomes is a great aid to a successful career.

So how much change management is enough?

There is no universal answer to the question: how much change management is required on a project? It depends on the situation.

For some projects there is not even a question to answer. Building a satellite is a seriously complex task that needs strong project management, and probably a major *change control* challenge, but there is no people change to manage. On the other hand, in some situations the change activity can dominate. Consider a cultural change in a large organisation. There may be an initial project defining and communicating desired behaviours, but in an organisation of any scale, such work takes years of positive reinforcement and day-to-day management to achieve a sustained outcome.

Many projects sit between these two extremes. Launch a new product, set up a new division, relocate people between offices, implement new processes and business systems – these are both projects and changes. In these situations project and change managers should respect each other's discipline and work to bring together a synthesis of the relevant parts for that specific project.

When I talk about reaching out, I mean more than taking bits from change management and sticking them into the project plan. I mean seeing the problems of delivery from a different angle. The angle that does not just ask: 'How do I create these complex deliverables?' But asks: 'How can I ensure these deliverables drive sustained change?' This change does not just occur during the life of the project but goes on happening long after the project is finished and probably forgotten. This may require additional activities in the plan, but it can also lead to looking at the whole process of delivery from a different perspective.

Widening horizons

Project management is increasingly powerful and specialised. The days of the amateur project manager who runs the project because they happened to be given the task are over. We are a specialist profession but there are disadvantages to too much specialisation. There is an old joke which says that specialists are people who know more and more about less and less, until eventually they know everything about nothing. One of the challenges of the modern world is the tendency for greater specialisation to lead to different disciplines becoming separated. Often the best ideas come when people from different disciplines share thoughts and effect a synthesis of approaches. Bring experienced project and change managers into a room to work out how to approach a complex project and change challenge and the results can be innovative and amazing.

Project management has evolved and we should be proud of the way our discipline continues to develop. But pride risks insularity. The best project managers do not just learn about project management, but gain a deep appreciation of other disciplines that help managers in business deliver lasting improvements. Change management should be high on your list of things to know more about – it is a powerful and evolving discipline in its own right.

Project manager's checklist

- Project and change management are both important disciplines in delivering innovation and enhancements in business

- They should be seen as complimentary not competitors

- Project and change managers should work together to find ways they can combine to deliver change efficiently and effectively

---

case study

Working with other disciplines

Liz is an experienced project manager. She started her career working on IT projects. Whilst the projects she is involved in now often have a big IT element they are broader, including organisational change and other performance improvement disciplines.

'One of the interesting challenges of working as a project manager on performance improvement initiatives is working with other disciplines. As an IT project manager I worked with business analysts, designers, developers, testers and architects. The IT project space is pretty mature, and whilst there are sometimes issues over who is actually in charge, generally the different roles involved in IT projects understand the role of the project manager and know how to work with project managers.

'When it comes to performance improvement projects the situation is more complex. There are change managers, *lean six sigma* experts, process improvement specialists and so on. Sometimes it is easy to work with these different experts, but sometimes it can be challenging. Not all of them understand or accept the role of the project manager. And to be fair project managers don't always understand the role of other performance improvement disciplines.

'Resolving this problem is not just a matter of writing a *RACI chart*. That's the normal solution for project managers faced with a complicated project team and unclear responsibilities. In these situations you cannot simply write a RACI chart because the other roles see the world in different ways, use different terminologies and concepts, and many of the things I think are owned by project managers, they may want to own.

'This problem can be solved, but only by taking the time to sit down and work with other disciplines: to explain different models of how performance improvement initiatives can be organised and to try to see the world from each other's viewpoints. Once you have done this it usually becomes possible to structure an organisation in which you all have clear roles, accept each other's responsibilities and can work together harmoniously.'

From delivery to benefits realisation

What is this about and why is it important?

Project management's core concern is the creation and implementation of deliverables. But organisations do not make an investment in projects for the sake of deliverables. Project investments are made to enhance the organisation by enabling benefits to be realised.

Projects enable benefits, but usually they do not directly realise them. Projects create deliverables: new IT systems, processes, buildings and facilities, new products and so on. It is the exploitation of the deliverables which creates benefits. Occasionally, benefits arise during the life of the project, but normally they occur afterwards. These may seem to be pedantic points, but they are important.

Just because a project hands over all the expected deliverables it does not mean that the anticipated benefits are delivered. The history of projects is full of examples of apparently successful projects which delivered few benefits. Yet there is little point in undertaking projects unless benefits are realised.

This section looks at some of the challenges in *benefits realisation*, and the approach to take to ensure benefits are realised.

Objectives

- To ensure that projects realise benefits
- To provide an approach for better benefits management

Common issues in achieving these objectives

- Lack of emphasis on benefits realisation
- No responsibility allocated for, or mechanisms to track, achieving benefits
- Split accountabilities for project delivery and benefits realisation, combined with insufficient agreement and handover between parties involved

The guide

In this section, I start by defining three problems which impede benefits realisation. Then, I discuss how to ensure benefits are realised.

Problem 1: the project managers' approach

As might be expected from a big varied community, project managers have different approaches to benefits management. The approaches project managers take tend to reflect the culture and behaviour of managers in the organisations they work in.

The worst case is when no consideration is given to benefits. This is increasingly rare, but does occur. More common is that a project concept is developed and decided upon, and then a business case is developed to justify the project. There is little follow-up or checking that benefits are realised later on.

It is better to develop the business case before deciding to undertake the project, with some form of defined *benefits tracking* process to follow on after the project. Best of all is when the benefits management process is tightly ingrained into the project approach. Few project managers do this.

An additional problem arises: projects keep changing as they progress. These may be formal changes reflected in *change requests*. It may be issues arising which cause delays and require action to resolve. It can be *risks* being realised which negatively effect the project. If these things happen, they can impact benefits. Yet often the business case is not updated as the project changes.

Benefits are relative to costs. For a project to be worthwhile it obviously has to deliver greater benefits than it costs. To be sure of this we have to know the cost of the project. Many projects run without properly tracking costs. Even if a nominal cost assessment is developed up front, on many occasions costs are not tracked. The real cost of projects – the actual cost of the time that all resources spend on the project – is not measured or understood. Hence the business case is wrong.

Problem 2: measurement

Another key problem with benefits management lies in the area of measurement. There are many difficulties in identifying and measuring benefits.

Most obviously, there may be a lack of measures. Some important benefits are intangible. But even if a benefit is theoretically measurable there may be no history or baseline. If there is no baseline you cannot tell how much a project has improved on this baseline and what the realised benefits are.

Many projects are justified because of their strategic alignment. This sounds great, as businesses should invest in the projects with the best strategic alignment. Unfortunately, there is a tendency to define projects as strategic to avoid having to define any other benefits than alignment to strategy.

Alternatively, there can be a sole emphasis on financial measures. Financial measures are easy to quantify, and comparatively easy to measure. This ease of use can result in an exclusive focus on finance, to the detriment of other benefits. Many useful and valuable projects may be ignored because of a lack of a financial business case.

Even if all benefits can be measured theoretically, this will only happen if the tools and mechanisms for measurement are in place, and someone actually does the measurement. Many projects do not account for this need.

Problem 3: cashing the cheque

The third set of problems relate to actually realising the benefits a project has delivered – known colloquially as 'cashing the cheque'.

One significant reason why this issue is common is that projects are detached from those who must deliver the benefits. *Stakeholders* are surprised when a project completes and they are expected to deliver benefits from it, or they simply refuse to acknowledge the reality of the benefits the project has enabled.

It can be hard to realise some benefits – especially small incremental ones. For example, consider a project which delivers a performance improvement of one hour per week across a pool of 1000 staff. Assuming the staff typically work 40-hour weeks, this means that the organisation could continue to do the same work with 25 fewer staff. Whilst the arithmetic is obvious, identifying the staff to make redundant is much harder.

Sometimes benefits may be enabled by projects without a link to the annual budgeting process. If a project reduces costs by 10%, but all budgets are the same next year as this year, no benefit is likely to be realised.

Finally there is the issue of competition between projects for the same benefits. Two projects may offer benefit of level 'x' in some aspect of the business – but a cumulative benefit of '2x' is never achieved. This double counting of benefits is common. When assessments are made of the total benefits across a *portfolio* of projects they may be greater than possible, and regularly greater than delivered.

Designing projects for benefits

It need not be like this. Benefits realisation is never going to be simple or non-contentious. Measurement of benefits can throw up some intractable problems. However, it is quite possible to improve benefits realisation significantly.

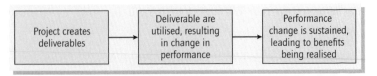

Linking projects to benefits

Benefits realisation starts in the prioritisation and *portfolio management* processes. These determine the choice and resourcing levels of projects. This should be based on a clear understanding of benefits as defined in project business cases, with efforts to remove any double counting.

Project *sponsors* should start with the right attitude towards benefits: not 'This is what I want to do – now how do I justify it?', but 'Here's the area we need benefits in – so what projects should we do?'

An early step for projects is the development of a business case. The thinking around a business case should not just consider theoretical benefits, but also the practical realisation of them. At the outset of the project, consider how benefits will be measured, who does the measurement, and who is accountable to deliver them. Stakeholder buy-in should be gained up front, not in the latter stages of the project.

What is measured should have a baseline representing the state at the start of the project. If there are no measures or no *baseline plan* these must be delivered as part of the project, and ideally at a very early stage of the project.

As the project progresses business cases should be maintained that consider the impact of changes, risks and issues. Stakeholders must be kept engaged and holding onto a sense of ownership of the benefits as they modify. True project costs should be accurately tracked.

Projects can be planned to optimise the delivery of benefits quickly. There is generally an advantage in achieving benefits early because of the time value of money. If benefits have to be delivered in-year the speed to benefit becomes even more important.

Projects should be primarily designed and managed for benefits. Once a project is complete the delivery of benefits should continue to be measured. This measurement checks success, and drives the behaviour to ensure benefits are realised.

Most important of all is the behaviour and culture of the organisation. Managers should seek to develop a culture of accountability for benefits, where stakeholders are held accountable for the delivery of benefits long after the project has completed.

Project manager's checklist

- Projects are undertaken to deliver benefits

- The practice of benefit realisation is harder than the theory

- The behaviour of project managers and sponsors, difficulties with measurement and problems with ensuring that benefits are realised, means that benefits are often not achieved

- By designing and managing projects for benefits, and by ensuring clear responsibilities for tracking and delivering benefits, these problems can be moderated

The lessons from lean and six sigma

What is this about and why is it important?

The world of management thinking is always coming up with new ways of enhancing organisations. The cynic thinks of these as fads, and some of them are, but others make fundamental long-term improvements.

Two of the biggest trends in management have been the adoption of *six sigma* and *lean*. These were originally separate approaches, but they are often conflated nowadays into lean six sigma. In this section I will treat them as one discipline, although in reality both lean and six sigma bring different tools, areas of focus and value.

Whilst I do not see lean six sigma as a panacea for all business problems, as some of its staunchest advocates present it, it has proven to be of value. Lean six sigma is not exactly leading-edge thinking anymore, but it has powerful lessons for project managers and project teams which are new to many practitioners.

Objectives

- To understand the lessons from lean six sigma as applied to *project management*
- To encourage practitioners to look beyond traditional project management for lessons, tools and techniques

Common issues in achieving these objectives

- Lack of awareness, understanding or belief in lean six sigma
- Sticking with known approaches and unwillingness to try something new

The guide

Lean six sigma is a powerful approach, with a wide range of tools which need far more space to describe than a short section can encompass. Rather than try to make you a lean six sigma expert, I want to look at some of the underlying philosophies of lean six sigma, and show what project managers and teams can learn from this.

Lesson 1: start with the customer

Lean six sigma puts customers and customer satisfaction at the heart of everything it does. It starts by considering the needs of the customers (the voice of the customer), and defining quality in terms of the customer. Lean six sigma seeks to improve customer satisfaction, reduce defects (anything unacceptable to a customer), reduce waste (non-value-adding activities), and reduce cycle times. Good is not good enough; quality can always be improved further.

What is the lesson for projects? The best projects have a relentless focus on customers, but all too often customers are treated as people who are spoken to at the start and end of the project: in between they are forgotten. On a daily basis there is no questioning of 'How is what I am doing adding value to the customer?' Only work which progresses towards outcomes of real customer value, or reduces the *risk* of achieving them, should be included in the project.

Lesson 2: the importance of data

Lean six sigma is a fact-based discipline with an obsessive focus on data. Of course, in many situations there is inadequate data to understand situations and measure improvements. When this is true, lean six sigma does not just accept this, but finds measures – whether this is by counts, samples or other approaches.

In lean six sigma you cannot claim a benefit unless you have a baseline to measure against, and much of the training in lean six sigma is on measurement and data analysis. But not just any data will do, it has to link back to the customer's needs.

Some projects are brilliantly analytical, but the lesson for other projects is clear. Drop those weak business cases with half-thought-through metrics, immeasurable claims and unproven benefits. If there are no measures in place, early in the project put them in place and build your baseline to show progress against them.

Lesson 3: challenging the iron triangle

One central piece of project management thinking is the 'iron triangle' – stating the interdependency between time, cost and quality. The theory is that you cannot alter one without having an impact on the others. For instance if you reduce project time then you must either increase cost or reduce quality.

The iron triangle was a brilliantly clear and insightful piece of thinking by its inventor, Dr Martin Barnes. It is a helpful way of thinking about projects, and a powerful tool for working with project *stakeholders* explaining why their requests in one area have an impact elsewhere. But the iron triangle is not a law. Indeed it has been criticised by some as being too simplistic – but I like its simplicity, again as long as it is not treated as a law.

Many lean six sigma initiatives have shown that it is possible to reduce cost, increase speed and increase quality. By removing waste, focusing only on value-added tasks, and by reducing defects, processes can be improved in all three dimensions at once.

Does this mean I do not use the iron triangle? No, but I treat the iron triangle as a useful, but at best partially true, model. If you apply the iron triangle as a law to your project it assumes you have perfectly planned it, you have chosen approaches which have no waste and only do value-added tasks, and that you have a negligible defect level. I have found few projects like this. In most projects there is room to improve our project management practices, processes and tools to eliminate redundant steps and improve quality.

This is not just a theoretical point. Simple steps like reducing work-in-progress (as done in *agile*), can improve cost, time and quality. There may be a trade-off between these dimensions, but only once you have perfected your project approach!

When challenged to decrease time, cost and quality, do not forget the iron triangle as it may hold true, but be open to thinking about and finding alternative, lower-waste and lower-defect project practices.

Lesson 4: learning

Lean six sigma is built on a learning and continuous improvement model. Coaching is inbuilt. There is formal training, lots of it, but as important is the on-the-job coaching that goes on throughout lean six sigma projects. Master black belts coach black belts, who in turn coach green belts, who in turn work with and coach team members. The whole thing self-replicates: every lean six sigma initiative adds value in its own right, but also coaches a wider pool of lean six sigma team members. This is a great model for improving and expanding project management skills.

Lean six sigma assumes the best people to fix a problem are the people who do the work day in, day out. The *assumption* is that the team knows the problems and can find answers. Lean six sigma is not about micro control of how work is done – it is about micro control of the outcomes from work.

Many project managers could learn from this. There is a tendency to focus on controlling the activities and approaches team members use. A more productive focus is to ensure that a relentless focus on outcomes is being achieved, combined with an attitude of coaching team members to find ways of solving project problems themselves.

In project management we talk about learning and continuous improvement, but too often this is left to the luck of on-the-job training and a cursory post-implementation review. There is nothing wrong with on-the-job learning, as long as it is orientated to real learning needs and supported by appropriate coaching. Post-implementation reviews are powerful learning opportunities, as long as learning really is achieved. But learning can also be a deliberate daily part of a project's routine: what is going well, what is getting in the way, and what can be done differently.

(See p. 55 for the benefits of this learning focus on high-performance teams and p. 231 for learning and continuous improvement on projects.)

Project manager's checklist

Lean six sigma provides some powerful lessons for project managers and project teams, including:

- have a relentless focus on the customer

- be fact based

- understand the limits of the iron triangle – in many situations you can simultaneously improve time, cost and quality

- build learning into everything you do

eight

Aligning projects to business needs

Projects exist within a context, and for most of you that context will be a business or other complex organisation. A well-run project has a clear set of objectives, but these objectives are often set at the micro level of the individual project. Outside of the project there is a larger set of objectives or strategy that the organisation as a whole is trying to achieve. An individual project's objectives may or may not be aligned to these corporate objectives – but irrespective of this they cannot be ignored. This part considers four typical contemporary business challenges that set a context in which projects operate.

The first section looks at the need to deliver a project quickly. We live in a world that seems to go faster and faster – project managers cannot ignore this challenge and it means that projects must go faster too. If speed was the only challenge project managers might find life easier, but it is not. Many projects not only have to go faster, but are being delivered in cost-constrained environments in which every penny counts. The mantra 'faster-cheaper-better' is the norm. This is the topic of the second section. The third section considers optionality in projects. Organisational strategies and business needs often change faster than projects can be delivered. One answer to this is trying to keep options open in projects for as long as possible. The final section looks at how far projects need to go in terms of consideration of stakeholder needs. In the era of corporate social responsibility, what is a project responsible for?

High-speed project management

What is this about and why is it important?

Most project managers and project team members have presented a well-thought-through project plan, only to get the response from *sponsors* and customers – can't you do it any quicker? Looking from the opposite direction are sponsors and customers who have reviewed a project roadmap and felt it meets their requirements except for the time the project will take.

There are different reasons why projects are asked to go faster. Sometimes it is just part of that instinctive management response to ask for everything to be quicker and cheaper. Often it reflects a real need. Perhaps, a commitment was made before the project was planned. More generally, there is increasing pressure to innovate and make changes faster. One of the main engines of innovation and change is projects.

Objectives

- To understand the ways in which projects can be delivered faster
- To help project teams reduce project duration
- To support management in making realistic commitments based on real business needs

Common issues in achieving these objectives

→ Insufficient partnership between project teams and management in making compromises to meet time challenges

→ Unrealistic and unachievable commitments prior to project planning

→ Poor project planning

The guide

How can project teams, managers and sponsors respond to the need to go faster? There are three questions to consider:

1 How can you avoid the problem in the first place?
2 How can the project team speed up the project?
3 How can sponsors and *stakeholders* assist in speeding up projects?

Avoid the problem

My first response to the need to go faster may seem like I am opting out of answering the question. But there is a real option – and that is to avoid the need to go faster in the first place. How can this be done? There are a couple of ways:

1 **Start the project earlier:** this is a serious point. Often the need to go faster is driven by delays in starting a project. The end date of a project may seem a long time away, until a plan is actually drawn up. Do not fall into the mañana trap when it comes to starting projects. Start as soon as you can. A useful way to speed the initiation of a project is to actively manage the process of authorisation and buy-in.

2 **Set expectations and manage commitments:** often there is no real business need to deliver quickly beyond a senior manager's commitment and a desire to avoid embarrassment. Minimise the *risk* of over-eager commitment making by continuously and actively managing the expectations of senior managers. This will not stop overly optimistic commitment making completely – but it can help to reduce it over time.

Avoiding the problem will not work in all, or probably even most, situations – but it is worth exploring. It is most relevant when you repeatedly deliver projects for one customer. By entering into dialogue about timescales at the start of every project you can, over time, influence the customer's thinking about projects and modify the way they make commitments.

Project team actions

If you cannot avoid the problem then the project team have an issue to deal with. The project team have several options in this situation.

I am going to avoid the obvious comments such as work harder or longer hours. It is not that such things do not work, but they are not long-term solutions. Removing a few days or weeks from a project timeline can be done by working harder, but this will not resolve the situation of a continuous and repeated need to speed up projects. Similarly, more aggressive management can make a project go faster – especially if you have a lethargic project team – but it will only work for so long.

One answer is to think creatively about the project approach. There is no simple set of guidelines for this, but often projects are designed around a way a project team has worked in the past. There may be innovative alternatives to reduce duration – think, research and ask other project managers.

Other options the project team should consider to reduce duration include:

- **Reduce requirements and scope:** generally when a commitment is made the expectation is that a project will deliver. There is often more flexibility about precisely what it will deliver. Reducing *scope* and removing 'nice-to-have' requirements can shorten timescales considerably.

- **Increase parallel tasking:** if a project has several tasks planned in series, then the elapsed time of a project can be reduced by greater parallel tasking. (This is sometimes called *project crashing*.) But tread with care, as this in turn increases resource usage and management complexity. The classic book by Frederick Brooks, *The Mythical Man-Month: Essays on Software Engineering* (Addison-Wesley, 1995) has shown the folly of simply assuming that adding resources will speed up a project.

- **Ensure individual resources are minimising multi-tasking:** this may seem to conflict with the previous point, but it does not. Parallel tasking across a project does not mean that individual team members need to multi-task. Whilst it may seem counter-intuitive, minimising multi-tasking can increase the speed of a project (see p. 113).

▪ **Break the project into short deliverable cycles:** this is essentially what *agile* does. It may not speed the completion of all desired deliverables, but it does provide incremental value quickly by regularly delivering small enhancements (this in turn gives customers greater faith in a project and an increased tendency to support it).

▪ **Reduce dependencies:** the duration of a project is driven by the sequence of the tasks that needs to be done, which in turn is determined by the sequence these tasks must be done in – in other words the chain of dependencies. Before accepting the elapsed time of any plan, review all dependencies to check that none of them can be removed. In most cases you will find that some of them can.

▪ **Take greater risk:** have you been too conservative in the way you planned your project? Deliberately increasing risk should be done with care. Yet projects are inherently risky and project managers should not simply avoid risk – but manage it.

Sponsor and customer actions

The reality is that project teams can only do so much to speed up projects without reference to the sponsor or customers for decisions or compromises on the project. When we consider the actions that this wider group can take to reduce project duration, there are two separate types. There are things that could be done to all projects in an organisation's *portfolio*, but there are also ways to speed up projects by favouring them over others (i.e. 'robbing Peter to pay Paul').

How can sponsors help in reducing the time of all projects in a portfolio? Well they can support the project team by minimising scope and deliverables to the essentials. If you look carefully it is surprising how much are optionals or nice-to-haves rather than project essentials.

Sponsors can also help project teams to limit stakeholder numbers. Multiple stakeholders can increase the non-productive time of a project team. Reducing the number of stakeholders to take requirements from, manage and generally deal with can increase a project's pace.

What can be done to favour one project over others?

- **Prioritisation:** the simplest, and often most effective way of speeding up a project is to prioritise it higher – as long as your prioritisation system really does work (see p. 131). If you are going to do this, you must be honest. Making something faster in this way means something else must go slower. If you do not accept this you are paying lip service to prioritisation.

- **Re-align resources:** the best resources tend to be significantly more productive than the average – and so faster. Alternatively, team members could have any additional work removed so they are dedicated to a project. Or there is the simple approach of just adding more resource but this obviously has a cost penalty (see my comments on increasing parallel tasking above, as this does not always work). This is most likely to work early in a project's life.

Shortening project timescales in practice

What I have tried to do in this section is to give a flavour of the variety of tools at a project team's disposal when faced with the challenge of speeding up a project. The answer rarely lies in any one of these options, but is usually achieved by a combination of them. Whatever combination is used the real answer lies in project teams designing their project for speed. If a project has to be done quickly, then the speed of delivery should be considered in every decision that is made, and every element of the project plan.

Start by running a workshop where a broad set of project team members come together and review plans and identify approaches to find ways to speed the project up.

Project manager's checklist

- Go faster/deliver quicker are common challenges for project teams

- One response is to avoid the problem in the first place by starting earlier or controlling management commitment making

- The project team have a range of tools to reduce project duration. Review the plans and approach and see which tools can be applied in your situation

- The project sponsor and stakeholders have a significant role to play in reducing project durations – both for all projects in a portfolio, but also by prioritising urgent projects

Delivering in a cost-constrained environment

What is this about and why is it important?

There is always less money available in organisations than the total desired. Projects are often allocated less money than planning has determined is needed. Additionally, business projections and economic conditions alter, resulting in budget amendments. Project budgets are reduced after project plans based on those budgets have been committed.

These are not occasional challenges for project managers. Small and regular budget reductions are an ongoing reality for many project teams.

Objective

- To help respond to the challenge of reducing project costs

Common issues in achieving this objective

- Poor planning and estimating
- Lack of innovative thinking
- Unstructured and poorly analysed responses to budget reductions
- Badly managed *stakeholder* perceptions

The guide

What costs?

If you are looking to reduce costs, be clear which costs you want to reduce. In our personal lives we tend to think of all money as the same, there is just one pot of it! In business there are different types of money. In different situations each of these types can come under different levels of pressure. Factors to consider are:

- **Accounting treatment:** are you squeezed on your capital costs (capex) or your operational costs (opex)? What are the capitalisation treatments of different aspects of the project? It is not unusual to have differing levels of pressure on opex and capex. Unless you understand what counts as what, you may cut costs in areas you do not need to, or not cut enough where you do.

- **Budget periods:** if your project crosses budget years are you being asked to reduce the total project cost, or the amount spent this budget year? If it is the latter, one solution may be to delay work or purchases until next year. Sometimes the opposite is true; you can spend this year but not next. In this situation, speed becomes important and you must try to find ways to reduce project duration (see p. 179). Occasionally, total spend does not matter, but rate of spend does. In this case align plans to the rate of budget availability.

- **Which elements of your project finance are squeezed:** sometimes funding comes from multiple stakeholders, and not all of them have the same budget pressures. Although it is never popular, perhaps one group of stakeholders can pick up additional costs that other stakeholders can no longer afford. If the alternative is no project at all, some stakeholders may be willing to do this.

- **Project costs or impact of project on costs:** is it really just a cheaper project, or are the whole life costs of the deliverables from the project more important? (Also known as the total cost of ownership or TCO.) At times, you have to spend in a project to save costs in operations. If TCO must be reduced, sometimes increased rather than lowered project budgets are required.

Reducing the project cost

Let us assume you must reduce costs. Faced with this challenge, most project managers consider the iron triangle of *project management*. If costs are reduced something else has to give, either time or quality. The theoretical logic is unquestionable, but most of us have not planned with such absolute accuracy that there is a hard relationship between cost, time and quality. In other words, there is 'fat' in a plan.

Look for the fat. Challenge the project team. Go through the details of the plan. If there are any impact-free cuts that can be made they should be made. But you need to do this with a balanced attitude. You need to find the fat, but you also need to avoid removing the muscle or bone. If the project team do not complain at all, you probably are not pushing hard enough. If the project team are only complaining, you may be pushing too hard.

In cutting the fat, do not simply remove contingency from the plan. Fat is excess; contingency is a buffer against *risk*. If you are squeezed into reducing contingency, make sure your *sponsor* and stakeholders understand they are increasing project risk.

If you have cut the fat and still need to cut further, you have three choices:

1 **Reduce scope, requirements or quality:** review all your requirements. Normally, once there is no fat in the plan, the next step is to reduce what the project is delivering. Remove some deliverables or reduce the complexity of others. Look for lower-priority items to remove. I always prefer to reduce *scope* or requirements than to reduce quality. But often, a refusal to discuss reducing requirements in situations of less money simply results in lower quality.

2 **Cheaper resources:** are your resources cost effective? We can give up Champagne and drink Prosecco. However, never respond to cost reductions with a universal move to cheaper resources. Consider the project team members. Cheaper teams can actually result in more expensive projects. It is productivity that counts, not the day rate. The more expensive team members may be the most productive.

3 **Innovate:** find clever ways of doing things cheaper. Bring the team together and have a workshop to identify better

ways to deliver the project. Do not assume that the way you have planned is the only way. Doing this has a side benefit. Involving the team in cost reduction workshops helps to focus everyone's attention on costs.

If you start a project during tough times, consider and plan in options. Build your plan by considering what happens if the budget is reduced. Will the project still be able to deliver value (see p. 190)?

There is a cynical way to avoid the problem of reduced budgets: ask for more budget than you require, in the expectation the budget will be cut. I would be lying if I said this never works. Ignoring the ethics of doing this (which are questionable!), if you are caught out or perceived to be doing this, when the cuts come, you are likely to be hit hard.

Managing perceptions

When budgets are cut, rarely does the knife fall in an even-handed manner. Some areas have budgets cut hard, others remain relatively unscathed. What accounts for the difference in treatment? One factor is how closely the project aligns with organisational strategy. More strategic projects tend to fare better than those projects seen as peripheral to achieving the strategy. But what is 'strategically aligned' is not always clear and presenting the project as strategic can help.

Another factor is how the project is perceived by the wider stakeholder community. Are you seen as an essential project, or a nice-to-have? The nice-to-haves are often the first projects to be culled. Try to position your project as core, not peripheral. Are you seen as *lean* and mean already, or is there a perception that you are a gold-plated project? From the outset of your project always try to be, and set the perception that you are, budget conscious.

Another critical perception is whether your project is seen as part of the problem or part of the solution. If an organisation is trying to reduce costs, as a consumer of budget is your project just seen as a cost, or will your project deliver reduced costs or increased revenues? Even in the most savage budget reductions, most managers realise there are situations in which you must spend to save. If your project will lead to longer-term efficiencies, make sure you stress these at every opportunity.

Facing the truth

There are situations in which a project really is a nice-to-have. On these occasions, the best thing to do may be to put up your hand and suggest the project is culled. Resources can then be reallocated to more important projects.

Additionally, for most projects there is a minimum budget below which your project is not viable. If you are hitting these levels make clear to your stakeholders that it is not worth continuing the project. We are all better off pursuing projects that will lead to some benefit than striving to complete projects which deliver no value.

Project manager's checklist

- When costs are squeezed, determine which categories of cost must be reduced

- When project costs must be reduced, first cut any fat, then look for specific reductions

- Budget reductions do not fall evenly. Manage perceptions to help your project survive

- Do not push on regardless. If budgets really are too small, stop the project

Optionality in projects

What is this about and why is it important?

Change is ongoing for most organisations. Strategies alter due to innovations, inventions, technical advances, competitor activity and the evolution of social behaviours and expectations. Unforeseen operational problems arise which cause modifications to priorities. All of this, and more, affects projects.

It is easy to identify with common scenarios: a business strategy changes significantly, a project's budget is drastically reduced, there is a major change in business priorities, a customer decides to radically alter project requirements, or a project's business case depends on *assumptions* which are found out to be wrong.

Most project managers are well aware of these types of *risk* but the impact on specific projects varies. At one extreme, projects become unviable or irrelevant as such changes unfold, at the other extreme projects continue unaffected. For most projects, reality lies in the middle.

Many project managers ignore these risks, or think of them at the beginning of a project and write a list of assumptions, and then behave as if they can wash their hands of the problem. In some situations this is the right approach. But in others it is not and *project management* has resources to plan for and deal with such scenarios.

Objectives

- To help project managers think about project optionality
- To design plans which can adapt to radical changes

Common issues in achieving these objectives

→ Rigid adherence to defined *scope* and requirements

→ Fixed rather than managed assumptions

The guide

The traditional model

Traditional projects start by specifying project scope and requirements in detail. These are then used as the basis for the project which progresses on the assumption that these will not change. Should change in scope or requirements occur then there is the *change control* process. Change control provides a way to assess changes and then re-plan and re-budget a project based on the changes.

The experience of change control is not a happy one for many project customers. By fixing requirements it removes uncertainty from the project, but this is of little value to the customer who still has changing needs. In some situations, pursuing a project in this way simply ignores the customer's real need and situation. Flexibility is not just a nice-to-have, it is essential.

Nevertheless, this traditional model has many virtues and has proved successful as the basis to deliver many projects, and will continue to do so. It forces customers to think through their needs and intentions. By providing clarity it facilitates good planning, estimating and management commitment making. But there are some situations in which volatility and uncertainty are significant, and for which the rather blunt tool of a fixed requirements specification combined with a change control process is not a satisfactory answer.

Options

The alternative approach to rigid requirements supported by change control is to try and build some flexibility into a project.

The world of corporate finance has developed the concept of options analysis. An option is the ability to make a choice at a future date, and options analysis is based on the realisation that such options have value. Running a project such that project customers have flexibility has value for those customers. This value can be quantified.

There are many situations in which considering future options is not worth the effort. I would not suggest that you plan for every eventuality on every project but that you consider options for some projects. These projects have certain characteristics:

- They are doing something which is of exceptional importance or value to your organisation.
- They exhibit a high degree of uncertainty.

In options analysis the value of an option is related to the level of uncertainty and the value of the underlying asset. In our case that asset is the project outcome. It is in high-value, high-uncertainty projects that it is most worth considering options.

If your project has a very short lifetime, of days, weeks or a few months, considerations of optionality are usually irrelevant. However, this is sector specific. Some businesses exhibit extreme uncertainty even in a short timescale.

If your project has a long duration, especially those that last several years, it is likely that the project will have to deal with significant changes. For large *programmes*, it is impossible to predict the budget available, the requirements, or the business situation in several years' time with any certainty. It is not just that people are not good at predicting, the whole idea that you can make accurate predictions in such situations is questionable (see p. 142).

Building in flexibility

There is not just one way to build in flexibility, nor is there one possible outcome for a project. Different approaches have differing costs, but also provide differing options to project customers who may be willing to pay more for a project that keeps options open for longer.

The main point is that to deliver optionality in a project it must be designed to provide options. A few aspects of project design that can impact the available options include:

- **Deferring projects:** the simplest solution to an unknown is to defer a project until it becomes known. This should not be discounted, but in many situations the length a project takes makes it essential to start before all information can be known.

- **Plan delivery to the boundary of predictability only:** rather than large programmes trying to predict the state a long time in advance, deliver in short chunks around what is known. This is the approach *agile* takes, with short *sprints* based around committed *stories*, with the option to review and revise stories when the next sprint starts. The next sprint may begin in a few days' or in a week's time. Even a *waterfall* project can be structured into phased deliveries leaving the more uncertain aspects until later. The important point is that the sprint or phase must deliver something of value to customers, so if they decide to do something different the project has still been worthwhile.

- **Decision points:** plan the project around the uncertainty and try to leave key decisions as late as possible in the project's *lifecycle*. So rather than planning around delivery milestones, plan around decision milestones. The balance is to find ways to progress with what is certain, whilst delaying elements of the project until later.

- **Pursue multiple options:** instead of choosing an option to deliver the project, run parallel streams delivering alternative outcomes and deliverables. This is obviously an expensive option, but if you do a full options analysis calculation you may find it is worthwhile.

Deliverable flexibility

Another aspect of optionality is not about the project approach, but about the deliverables from the project. Project deliverables tend to be designed to meet the requirements collected for that project. Yet it is almost universally predictable that as soon as the project is complete adaptations may be required.

It is possible to design in flexibility from the outset. Deliverables are not designed just to be perfect for today, but are designed with the future in mind. Of course, you may not know what the precise changes will be, but you will know some areas that will definitely change. For example, in projects to deliver new products, it is usually certain that the price will change and more product features may be added. Hence there is a need for pricing and feature flexibility.

The ability to design in flexibility depends on the nature of the deliverables and is a specialist skill. Insisting that deliverables are designed with future flexibility in mind is hugely valuable in terms of cost and speed to deliver future options.

Project manager's checklist

■ Traditional project techniques fix requirements and manage change with a change control process. This enables the project to be delivered, but it often fails to meet real customer needs

■ There is value in optionality in projects, especially if the project is of high value and is operating in an environment of uncertainty

■ Projects can be designed with optionality in mind. In some cases this increases project budgets, but this can often be shown to be worthwhile if the true option value is assessed

■ Additionally, deliverables can be designed to respond flexibly to future as well as current needs

Giving options in projects

*Peter is a programme director working in the telecoms industry.
He runs a central project management team for a large telecoms
company, and has a background in engineering and operations as well
as project management. He talks here about options in projects.*

'One of the difficulties of working on really big projects and
programmes is deciding the outcome from a project a long time
before the project will be delivered. This is challenging because the
world moves much quicker than projects can progress. Often by the
time you get to the end of the work, what you started out to do is no
longer what is useful for the business. Additionally, when you start
you don't have all the information you need to decide what is the best
project outcome – this only becomes clear as the project progresses.
I've seen lots of brilliant projects fail because they deliver solutions to
yesterday's problems.

'One answer to this is to only run short and quick projects. We do a
lot of this and it helps, but there are some projects that are inherently
big and take a long time. The question is – how can we decide what
to deliver for tomorrow when we don't know what tomorrow will be
like?

'The answer is not to decide!

'I know this sounds like I'm dodging the question, but often on
projects we try and make a perfect design for the future when we do
not need to. We can leave options open by making decisions as late
as possible, instead of project manager's typical preference of as early
as possible! Additionally, whilst we do not know tomorrow's needs
exactly, we have a pretty good idea of what range of things will be
needed. So, we work on several things in parallel, aware that we will
not follow all of them through to the end.

'This of course has a cost associated with it. But if you work out when
you must make decisions and also work out the value of keeping your
options open, this is a cost that often can be justified.'

Who has a valid interest in the project?

What is this about and why is it important?

Projects have customers. Typically, the customer has a set of requirements and some money. A project is set up which spends the money to fulfil the requirements. As long as the project really does fulfil the requirements and spends no more than the allocated money everyone is happy.

Well that is the theory. The real world is more complex. As well as the customer, usually there are a range of other *stakeholders* who have differing interests in a project. There are good reasons for considering the interests of this wider group of stakeholders. If you do not, projects can struggle to deliver, deliverables may be less successful and business cases may be unachieved. Additionally, a project may have unintended negative impacts on unconsidered stakeholders. In the worst, albeit rare, cases, projects can result in legal disputes, social disruption or negative impacts on brand integrity because of unforeseen stakeholder dissatisfaction.

Considering stakeholders is not just about removing negative *risk*, it is also about identifying extra *opportunities*. Taking account of stakeholder interests may provide opportunities to ease projects, improve deliverables and enhance outcomes.

This is a fundamental issue which also links to the definition of *scope* and requirements of projects (see pp. 26 and 33), *risk management* (see p. 94), how you review projects (see p. 122), as well as wider *governance*, health and safety, regulatory, compliance, corporate social responsibility (CSR) and ethical responsibilities.

Objectives

- To understand whose interests you need to take into consideration in a project
- To take adequate account of those interests

Common issues in achieving these objectives

→ Pressure to deliver projects in limited budgets and timescales

→ Tendency to focus on obvious stakeholders and paying customers only

The guide

Some terminology

To discuss this topic it is helpful to have some terminology to refer to different groups of interested parties. In the interests of brevity, I will keep my lexicon short. My definitions may be contentious, especially my definition of customer, but they are sufficient for this section. In this section, the terms used for the different groups are:

- **the project:** the project itself, the project manager and project team;
- **the customer:** the individual or organisation paying for a project and defining the need (the *sponsor* is usually a representative of the customer);
- **stakeholders:** anyone who has the ability to influence the outcome of the project or is influenced by it.

The issue

At one extreme a project only needs to consider the interest of the direct customer – the person paying the bill. After all, if you pay for something you expect your interests to be primary. But often, for projects, this view is too narrow. At the other extreme, a project needs to consider the interests of all stakeholders. But if we accept the definition of a stakeholder I have just given, this can be too wide.

The issue boils down to a question: what is a sufficiently broad view of the relevant stakeholder community? From the answer to this question we then have to make decisions such as what priority we give to the interests of directly delivering a project, versus the interests of others in the organisation, versus the interests of the wider community. A balanced approach is needed, but how can we find the right balance?

Examples

To make this easier to understand, here are a few examples of the results for insufficient consideration of wider stakeholder interests:

- A project is planned requiring resources from another department. The project manager assumes the resources will be available. At the same time that department is reducing budgets and wants to remove these resources from the organisation.
- An IT system is deployed. One group of essential users cannot use the deliverables. They do not have the capability to do so as training was not included in the project's scope.
- A new set of equipment is designed for a production line. When implemented there is unexpected operational disruption and an increased level of operational cost.
- A new product is launched. It sells, but it could have sold much better if a few additional features were added that a key customer segment requires.
- A business process is changed. The new process breaches regulation and results in bad publicity for the organisation involved.

Most of the interests we need to consider for most projects are internal to an organisation, but in some cases external interests must be considered because the project has social, environmental or other impacts upon the community an organisation interacts with. Laws and regulations exist to ensure that interests we may not otherwise consider are accounted for.

Exploring this issue

Project management has the practice of *stakeholder management* as the core mechanism for exploring this issue. A stakeholder assessment starts by identifying the interested parties in a project. A stakeholder assessment should be undertaken on every project of any scale or complexity.

Another step is to take advice, especially from other experienced project managers who have worked on similar projects. Additionally, most large organisations have a range of specialist advisers who will provide input on the needs of different stakeholder groups, including operations, regulatory advisers, lawyers, CSR specialists, and health and safety advisers.

The key mechanism to determine which stakeholders should and should not be included is project or *programme* governance. There are a number of aspects to governance, but one of the most important is to ensure that a project is taking account of the appropriate range of interests. This can be achieved by formal guidelines and checklists, but is most often achieved by those responsible for governance asking questions of the form: 'Have you considered…?', 'How does this impact…?' and 'How are you accounting for…?' .The classic example is for a senior manager to ask a project team: 'How will this project impact operations and the total cost of ownership?' Or a lawyer asking: 'Have you done a compliance check?'

There is a natural tension as every extra interest considered tends to add complexity, cost and risk to a project, but considering them may also reduce other risks and add opportunities and value.

Challenges

The picture I have painted is not without its own challenges. The main challenges to considering stakeholder interests are:

- a lack of awareness or visibility of stakeholders and interests;
- conflict between different areas of interest, especially between the needs of the customer and other stakeholders;
- insufficient budget, time or appetite to consider wider interests.

Overcoming these challenges in a reliable way is difficult, and unanticipated stakeholder response to a project is a significant factor in a project's risk. The best starting point is to be open, using common sense to think through who might have an interest in a project. Ask your peers, sponsors and *steering committee* for who else should be considered.

Project managers should look to understand stakeholders' interests as early as possible, ideally during scoping and planning phases. You can either take direct planned action to account for these interests, or you will assess them as part of risk management. Project teams should check they are compliant with any corporate guidelines, policies or rules. In practice, this can be hard as in many modern organisations there are simply so many. When uncertain take specialist advice.

When interests clash, or there is insufficient budget to consider or fulfil certain interests, keep track of them. Ask sponsors and steering committees to decide between interests. Prioritising between different stakeholder interests and deciding to fulfil one set of needs over another are topics for those with governance responsibilities to determine, and should not be decided purely by a project team.

Project manager's checklist

▨ Projects often create an impact upon a wider group of stakeholders than the project customer. Other stakeholders must be considered

▨ There are costs and risks to considering additional stakeholders, but also opportunities to achieve extra value

▨ A project must take a balanced approach to determining how wide a set of stakeholders should be considered

▨ Governance processes have a key role to play in determining this balance

Challenging projects

This part explores the environment in which projects run to look at four common challenging situations for project managers.

The first section looks at the difficulties and approach to taking over a project that has already been running for some time without a project manager. Initiatives often begin before they are shaped into projects and this creates specific challenges for the project manager. The next two sections look at different aspects of a poor understanding of objectives and requirements. A lack of clarity in project objectives and insufficient understanding of requirements are some of the commonest problems in projects. There are effective approaches to overcoming these problems – as long as you choose the right approach for the situation. Finally, we look at the challenges of trying to deliver a project whilst a major organisational change is underway. Organisational change is a regular feature of modern business life, and being able to continue to deliver whilst it is ongoing is a key skill for senior project and programme managers.

Taking over the project no-one is running

What is this about and why is it important?

Read any *project management* guide, or discuss project management processes, and there is normally one important *assumption* that is taken for granted: the project manager's work starts at the beginning of the project. Unfortunately, this is not always true.

I have often been brought in to run a project well after it began. A typical example is when an initiative has been started by a senior executive. The executive has made promises based on the success of initiative: when it will be finished, what will be achieved and so forth. A vague set of tasks or *objectives* has been agreed across this executive's management team. The managers individually get on with their own tasks, but there is no plan or only a high-level plan on a page (see p. 118), there is no co-ordination of activity, and the managers pursue their individual elements at their own pace. Worse, each manager has interpreted the original instruction and aims in their own way.

In such a situation a project manager has to take over a project which is being run by no-one.

Objectives

- To develop a structured approach to taking over a project no-one is running
- To rapidly bring the project into a controlled state and from there to successful delivery

Common issues in achieving these objectives

➤ Lack of clarity over project *scope* or objectives

➤ Insufficient or inappropriate resources

➤ Limited or unclear progress to date

➤ Unmanaged expectations and commitments, poorly aligned with the reality of the project

➤ Organisational politics

The guide

There is no universal answer to the question of how to take over a project no-one is running. It depends on the context and the state of the project. Typically, when I take over such a project, I adopt a gradualist approach to intervention, and this is described in this section. Occasionally, I have had to step in straightaway and stop everything before bringing control, but often this is politically counter-productive. Either way, the advice here needs to be tailored to your specific situation.

The timescales given here are indicative and based around a large *programme* which will run for 12–18 months or longer. For a smaller project, strategic control has to come much more quickly.

Taking the project over

Faced with an unstructured piece of work, the temptation is to run in all guns blazing and try to enforce structure quickly. The most obvious way of doing this is to stop the project completely, and then follow the normal project management steps: write a project brief, understand objectives and scope, develop a plan and so on. In some cases, stopping the project is necessary because it is using significant resources, and is delivering nothing or is at complete variance with business priorities.

However, stopping the project generally should be avoided for two reasons:

1 It halts what progress is being made. Poor progress is usually better than none.

2 It is often politically unacceptable to stop the project, rightly or wrongly.

The alternative to starting from scratch is to build a project management structure around the work that is already ongoing.

The mindset to adopt is to think in terms of a pair of lines. One line represents what the project should be doing; the other line represents what the project is doing. Your aim is to bring the lines together. Initially, the unmanaged project's line can be going in any direction – even rapidly diverging from where it should be. Your aim, in the short term, is for the unco-ordinated initiative, without ever stopping, to evolve into a disciplined project.

To achieve this go through the following steps in the order shown:

1 Establish objectives, scope and expectations.

2 Secure short-term control.

3 Achieve tactical control.

4 Attain strategic control.

Establish objectives, scope and expectations

The problem with projects of this nature is that it is often unclear what the project is trying to deliver and what has happened so far. You want to get to a position in which you understand the objectives and scope of the project very clearly, and the project team and *sponsor* have realistic expectations about what can be delivered.

Start by interviewing a range of people involved in the project. For guidance, pick any number between six and 10 interviewees depending on the project's scale and complexity. These are typically hour-long meetings when you should discuss where the project is, what the expected outcomes are, interviewees' views of the key problems and issues, and their personal perspectives on the project. I run as many of these as I need, stopping when I start to hear the same information from those interviewed.

Try to run these meetings purely as information collection. Make no changes to the project and avoid setting too many expectations. Explain that you will bring structure and direction to the project, but only when you understand it. Stress that you are not a miracle worker. Any good project manager can add value to an unstructured and complex piece of work with better planning and discipline. But you cannot convert the impossible into the possible. Finally, try to make the people you are talking to feel positive about what they have done so far. You want to improve things, not start a battle.

One of the interviews has to be with the executive running the initiative. What is critically important is to understand how flexible the project's goals are. There are various aspects to the goals. The most important are usually delivery timescales and outcomes expected.

The end goal from these interviews is a good understanding of the project and the context. Develop a simple statement of objectives and the scope. Do not worry if this is not 100% perfect. It is a *baseline plan* for everyone to comment on, before producing an agreed set of objectives and scope definition.

Normally, for political reasons the delivery date cannot slip, often because it has been externally committed to. But what has been promised at this date is less well defined. It is common to end up with a two-phase project:

1 Phase 1: delivering **something** for the originally agreed date. This is the political deliverable.

2 Phase 2: delivering what is really required at some later date. This is the real deliverable.

Secure short-term control

Having developed a scope definition, start bringing control to the project. The main problem with an in-flight project is that you do not have the luxury of planning before the work starts. You have to plan in parallel with delivering the project. Your aims in the first 2–4 weeks should be to ensure the following:

- Whatever activity is being undertaken is at least moving the project towards the desired objectives. Do not, at this stage, be too concerned whether it is doing it in the best way or right order. But stop anything that is directly contrary to achieving the objectives or is outside of scope. You want your lines to start to converge – not to keep diverging!

- People working on the project get used to working with a project manager and to using basic disciplines and reporting.

- Expectations are reasonable. It is the time to start warning the project's sponsor if you think the goals are not achievable. You will not know for certain yet, but you should at least start to have a feeling. If your feeling is not positive, start managing expectations more assertively.

Achieve tactical control

In the next month or so bring the project to a level of tactical control. In this phase your concerns should be to:

- **Build a better and fuller plan:** the most important thing is that the plan is realistic.

- **Set realistic planning timescales and expectations:** develop an unrealistic plan and you will soon be adrift from it and confidence in you as a project manager will decline.

- **Assess the key *risks* facing the project:** what can go wrong and how is it best dealt with?

- Start getting the team into the habit of having their **activity directed** and **progress measured** around the plan.

- Help the team **understand** that **the project management process adds value**.

One way to get the team working as a project team is to give them some quick wins. Usually in an unco-ordinated initiative there are some issues that have been floating around which are not complex to resolve, they just require bringing some people together and agreeing a common way forward. I try to find a few of these, even if they are not priority concerns. Resolving them builds faith in the project management process.

Attain strategic control

Over the following three months take strategic control. Your aim at the end of this phase is to have a fully functioning project that appears to anyone outside as if it has always been a well-run activity. You want everyone working as a fully disciplined project team. One of the best levers to do this is the simplest. Every 1–2 weeks progress is reported against the plan. People are asked to explain variances from the plan. This simple, traditional project management approach tends to develop a much greater focus on the initiative as a project. This is most effective if the sponsor actively participates in some of these sessions, at least to start off with.

In parallel with this, involve the team in *risk management*. You want to move the team beyond thinking about today's work to looking forward to what is coming up and what may get in the way. Implement better project communications. It is usually a sign of a well-controlled project when there is a disciplined, consistent and co-ordinated set of communications to all project *stakeholders*.

Project manager's checklist

▦ Start by establishing a clear documented definition of objectives and scope

▦ As soon as you get involved, start managing expectations as to what is and is not possible

▦ Incrementally take control of the project, bringing the direction and approach of the project in line with what is required

▦ Do not stop the project unless it is diverging from actual needs

case study

Recovering projects that did not start as projects

Eric is a project recovery specialist. He works for a major multi-national and gets involved in troubled projects all over the world. His role requires quickly deciding if projects which have gone wrong can be recovered, and if they can then swiftly bringing them back on track.

'Often, what I take over are what I call "accidental projects". That is pieces of work that started out with some good intentions and desire to complete, but were normally not formally designed as a project. The piece of work expands, starts to eat budgets and resources, and before long there is a major initiative underway which is out of control for no other reason than no-one is running it.

'Taking over such a project needs a careful approach: balancing decisiveness with not jumping to conclusions and trying to apply a rigid one size fits all approach. Project management can sometimes be a blunt instrument that in bringing structure and control causes upset, bad feelings and political issues if it is applied without care of the human factors.

'The most important thing for a project manager to do in these situations is to develop trust. If no-one trusts you, then it is very difficult to come in and take over live pieces of work and turn them into effective projects, as no-one will follow your lead. When you have trust, people will listen to you and work with you to shape amorphous activities into structured projects. Additionally, when people trust you they will forgive you the mistakes that you will inevitably make in these situations.

'Developing trust is all about your behaviour. You need to give the people you are working with a real sense that you want to do the best for them and the project. You need to give them confidence that whilst you do not have the answer to every question, you have an approach to getting the answers. You should make sure everyone knows that tough decisions will have to be made that not everyone will like, but that this is not based on personal issues, related to people's performance or a criticism of what has gone in the past – it's just that projects require certain ways of working.

'With trust, if you are a good project manager, you can work wonders. Without trust, even if you are a brilliant project manager, you will struggle to get people to work with you in a constructive way.'

Not seeing the wood for the trees

What is this about and why is it important?

We all know that projects can go wrong for many reasons. There are all sorts of *risks* and issues that every project faces. Some of these are unique to a project, but if you analyse the challenges facing multiple projects a pattern of common issues emerges. One of the surprisingly common challenges is that the *objectives* and the *scope* of the project are unclear. Without clear objectives and without an ambiguously defined scope, trouble is bound to occur.

Objectives

- Ensuring that the objectives and scope of a project are clear
- Understanding how to identify when there are problems with the objectives or scope
- Having an approach to clarifying objectives and scope

Common issues in achieving these objectives

- *Sponsors* who lack clarity of thought or have an inability to express themselves
- Multiple sponsors with incompatible needs combined with a project manager who does not have the ability to challenge this situation
- Rapidly changing business environments
- Pressure to make progress and be seen to be making progress
- Focus on details and forgetting the big picture

The guide

In theory, having unclear objectives and scope is a very basic mistake for a project manager. Yet I am often surprised by how commonly project managers, project sponsors and team members cannot, convincingly, tell me the objectives of the project they are working on. If we are honest, when we reflect on the projects we have all been involved with, we can all think of some that did not have completely clear objectives.

Why is this? There are a number of reasons, but they are best summarised by the English expression 'not seeing the wood for the trees': you become so focused on the details that you lose sight of the big picture.

Projects are full of details, and one of the skills of a good project manager is to be aware of sufficient detail. But understanding detail should never be done at the expense of losing sight of the overall rationale for and direction of the project.

The big picture logic of projects

There is a simple piece of logic I use in any delivery-related activity. This logic determines that certain key project questions should be answered in the following order:

1 Why are we undertaking the project? Answering this question enables you to define objectives.

2 What are the boundaries of the project? Answering this enables you to define scope.

3 What do we need to develop to achieve the objectives whilst remaining within scope? Answering this enables you to define the deliverables.

4 What actions need to be taken to develop the deliverables? From this you can progress on to resourcing and planning.

In reality, these simple questions hide a lot of complexity. Each question can spin off much more detailed analysis and requires different approaches and skills to answer. In some cases, under-standing the objectives and scope of a complex *programme* can be a project in its own right. It is also not simply a linear process of answering these four questions. There are feedback loops in which the answers to later questions may mean going back to revisit the answers to earlier ones: for example, trade-offs reducing the project's scope based on the resources available, and from compromises on scope to modifications to objectives. But nevertheless, this high-level set of questions, answered in the order shown, gives the project's 'big picture'.

We often become so focused on the complexity and details that we lose sight of this simple logical flow:

Objectives → Scope → Deliverables → Activity → Plan → Resources

Project managers may try to keep control of many individual activities in the plan, and forget to keep an eye on the objectives. Project team members get focused on today's activities and not the direction they are going in. Project sponsors become obsessed with progress and seeing deliverables and forget to ask 'Is it the right sort of progress and the most appropriate deliverables?'

Identifying flawed projects

No matter how well you understand your plan, unless you can trace what is in the plan back to your original objectives then the plan is flawed.

When I am asked to review a project I always start by enquiring: What are the project's objectives? And please explain the scope of the project? If a project manager cannot meaningfully answer these questions then I know the project is either in trouble or will be soon. It either means the project manager does not know it – which is obviously a problem – or the project manager cannot explain it. A set of objectives or a scope which cannot be explained are as good as useless. Additionally, if key project team members do not answer these questions, consistently with the project manager's answers, then I think the project is likely to be in trouble.

The reality is that it often takes an outsider (a consultant, a peer reviewer or a quality manager) to see that a project does not have clear objectives or scope. This is a problem I see time and time again and is one that all project managers understand. So why do we fall into this trap?

Falling into the trap

In the urgency to make progress, and probably just as important, to be seen to be making progress, we often jump into the project without being clear about objectives. We are all familiar with the reality of working in a business. Budgets are set and commitments made long before a project is planned. It can therefore seem that we just need to get on with delivering as soon as the project really starts. This is always a mistake. Unless you are clear about the objectives and have a complete and unambiguous scope it is unlikely that the project will be a success.

You do not just have to know the objectives at the start of the project, you must keep them in mind as you deliver. There is a tendency for projects to veer away slowly from original intentions. We have all seen a project completing a year or two after it began, apparently a success but not delivering the outcome that was expected at the start.

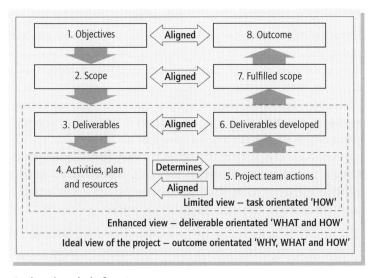

Seeing the whole forest

Of course, there are situations in which the objectives or scope are not easy to determine. Contributing factors include: uncertain, poorly communicating or distant sponsors; multiple *stakeholders* with different visions; a project manager who does not have the skills or is poorly positioned to challenge stakeholders; volatile business situations; projects which have been running for a long time and everyone has forgotten the original reason for starting them and so on (see p. 217).

The solution is not to progress the project in spite of this, but to see clarification of the objectives and scope as the first phase of the project. It is not until these are understood, that a plan and budget can truly be finalised. If objectives and scope have been forgotten or changed then they need to be *re-baselined* and the project plan amended accordingly. This can be painful on an in-flight project, but is essential for delivering real value.

If there are issues with objectives and scope that cannot be resolved, *assumptions* can be made. But it is critically important that these assumptions are managed as risks associated with the project. Additionally, the objectives and scope are key parts of the project you must maintain and keep under *change control*.

Occasionally a project is deliberately started when scope and objectives are unclear. If this is the situation, your first response should be to challenge the situation as often it reflects lazy thinking that is confusing volatile requirements with volatile objectives. There is a big difference between unclear or volatile requirements (which techniques such as *iterative* or *agile project management* are designed to handle) and unclear objectives. You can still have crystal clear objectives without clear requirements. Usually objectives are definable. However, occasionally a project really is a deliberate exploration into possibilities – it is simply a learning exercise.

If a project is designed to be an exploration, then structure it so that it is exploratory. Such exploratory projects need regular reviews of what has been found and how this impacts the scope and objectives. With exploratory projects the scope and objectives must become clearer over time otherwise the exploration is getting nowhere. Such exploratory projects are akin to map making, and like map making whilst you may start with a blank sheet of paper – the map needs to be filled in. If this does not start happening the project should be terminated.

Defining objectives and scope

The best way to determine objectives and scope is by structured questions; then documenting the result and getting it reviewed by the project sponsor and key project customers. (Read pp. 26, 33 and 217 for further ideas on how to achieve this.)

Project manager's checklist

- There is a straightforward logical flow in designing a project:

  Objectives —→ Scope —→ Deliverables —→ Activity —→ Plan —→ Resources

- A project manager should be able to answer, clearly, what the project's objectives are and describe the scope of the project

- Project sponsors and team members should understand the objectives and scope consistently with the project manager

- The project team should not only focus on the detailed work they are doing, but regularly check it is aligned with the project's defined objectives

- Where objectives and scope really cannot be concretely defined before starting a project then the project needs to be managed to account for this. If objectives and scope are not becoming incrementally clearer then stop the project

The customers who do not know what they want

What is this about and why is it important?

Two core *assumptions* underlie traditional *project management* approaches: the project customers know what they want, and they can define this. In reality, customers rarely know precisely what they want, and even when they do they often struggle to define it clearly and comprehensively to a project team. And yet how can a project be delivered if the customer cannot describe their requirements?

There are various techniques for determining customer needs. It is important that the right technique is used in the right situation.

Objectives

- To develop a clear and relevant understanding of the customers' wants
- To select the most appropriate project management approach and techniques depending on the degree to which a customer can define their wants

Common issues in achieving these objectives

→ Lack of clarity and volatility in requirements

→ Too many or non-compatible requirements

→ Forcing project progress with insufficient requirement definition

→ Inappropriate project management approaches and *lifecycles*

The guide

A brief taxonomy of customer wants

At the simplest level there is a hierarchy of customer wants. The first layer of this hierarchy is 'the why'. *The why* defines what it is that customers want to achieve through the project or the reason they want to do it. *The why* is defined in terms of **objectives**, **goals** or **benefits**. The next layer in this hierarchy is 'the what'. *The what* defines the specific outcome the client desires. This outcome is defined in terms of **deliverables**, and in more detail **requirements**. Some project management approaches replace the word deliverables with **products**. By utilising *the what* the customer will achieve *the why*. The final layer in this hierarchy is 'the how'. *The how* defines the way in which the project is performed and hence produces the deliverables. *The how* is defined in terms of **methods**, **lifecycles**, **approaches**, **processes**, **activities** and **tasks**. (For more detail see pp. 26 and 33.)

The why and *the what* are customer defined. *The how* is usually not, but there are situations in which the customer has to define how a project is performed. An example is organisations that must comply with statutory regulations on how certain projects must be performed.

Assessing the customers' understanding

To start you need to determine what it is that the customers do and do not know:

- Do they know and can they define *why* they want a project, with sufficient clarity?
- Do they know and can they define *what* they want from the project, in sufficient detail?
- Do they now know *how* the project is to be run, in the appropriate situations?

These are very different questions. Depending on which of them can and cannot be answered, and how they are answered, will dictate the project's approach.

The why

If a customer cannot define *why* they want a project, then as a project manager I am usually worried about the project. Without a clear definition of the objectives it is hard to run a successful project. It is common for customers to have a sense of the objectives, but not to be able to define them in clear, consistent terms. There are various solutions to this problem:

- **Documentation:** it sounds too simple to be true, but often just writing down the objectives as they are explained, and then sharing these with the customer, can encourage deeper thinking. This usually takes several iterations to finalise. The important point is that the documentation is a tool to get clarity – not an end in itself.

- **Business analysis:** one of the skills of a business analyst is to be able to determine and document the customer's reasons for having a project in a form that is clear and usable by a project team. A good business analyst is a blessing to a project.

- **Facilitated workshop:** an option is to run a facilitated workshop with the customer and project representatives. The output from this workshop is a defined set of objectives everyone understands and agrees to.

- **Exploratory project:** sometimes there are legitimate options and lack of clarity around objectives. This is the time for an initial exploratory project. This is usually a short project which delivers an options paper for a customer.

- *Governance*: important but sometimes forgotten aspects of project governance processes are to confirm and regularly review project objectives for ongoing relevance and clarity as projects progress.

These are not necessarily alternatives, but can be complementary approaches to clarifying objectives. It is essential, whatever approach or combination of approaches is chosen, that the overall objectives of a project are clear to all project *stakeholders* and team members. Without this, there is little guarantee that a project will head in the right direction.

The what

The key aspect of the customer requirements that usually causes problems is the definition of *the what*. Traditional project management approaches go through a very structured and formal process for describing deliverables, which are encapsulated in the *work breakdown structure*. Detailed customer requirements are then captured for each aspect of the deliverables.

Unfortunately, this conceptually simple breakdown of an outcome into deliverables, and from deliverables to detailed requirements, hides a huge amount of complexity. (The sad history of many IT projects shows the difficulties of extracting this information from clients.)

There are multiple reasons for, and solutions to, unclear requirements:

- The clients have not done the work to assess their requirements, or no-one has asked them to do so in a structured way. This is a straightforward issue, and can be resolved by suitable interviews and assessments by a business analyst. It is usually done at an early stage of the project.

- There are a complex set of stakeholders with differing wants and needs. This is also the job for a business analyst, combined with priority setting criteria agreed with the project *sponsor* or *steering committee*.

- The customers cannot know their requirements because they lack information, understanding or vision to be able to determine them. This is the situation in which prototyping or modelling projects helps. The purpose of the model or prototype is to explore and clarify options and possibilities, and from there agree requirements. The model or prototype is iteratively developed until it provides a full understanding of customer requirements. In some situations, such as software development, the prototype, after several iterations of development, becomes the final deliverable. Additionally, some customers can be helped to explore and define their requirements with the support of a subject matter expert who has been involved in similar initiatives in the past. This person can help customers understand options and advise on requirements.

▦ Requirements can never be known completely and are unstable because of volatility and regular change in the organisation or context of the project. In this situation, use short development cycles, which deliver what is known and stable and enable full customer requirements to emerge at the appropriate time. An ideal approach in this situation is *agile*.

The how

Generally, if a customer does not know *how* the project is to be run, I am not only unconcerned but positively happy. A key part of the role of the project manager, and any specialist resources on the project team, is to work out *the how* based on their assessment of the best way of achieving *the what* and *the why*. Too much interference from the customer in how the project is to be pursued is usually counter-productive and should not be encouraged, unless the customer happens to be an expert.

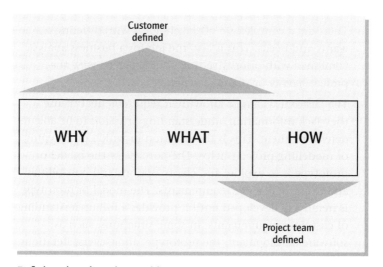

Defining the why, what and how

If there are specific reasons for the customer to define how the project is run, these should be elucidated at the start of the project from the appropriate subject matter experts.

Project manager's checklist

- Start by determining where the uncertainty lies. Is it in *the why*, *the what* or *the how?*

- Different types of uncertainty require different solutions to resolve

- Not knowing *the why* puts a project in jeopardy. Clarifying *the what* is usually part of the project. Customers usually do not need and should not be encouraged to define *the how*

- Modify project management approaches based on the customers' ability to define *the what*. If there is uncertainty, look to rapid prototyping or modelling projects. If there is volatility in requirements consider agile

Delivering in times of change

What is this about and why is it important?

There is an irony at the heart of many projects, especially business projects. Such projects are concerned with delivering change, but at the same time projects themselves operate best in an environment of stability and certainty. Yet stability and certainty are not consistent features of business. Effective project managers must learn to deliver projects in environments which are changing, even as this change impacts the project itself.

Sometimes, the level of volatility can be extreme. In this section I discuss an extreme: the situation of a major management re-organisation – or revolution.

Objective

- To continue to deliver appropriate projects whilst significant organisational change is going on

Common issues in achieving this objective

Trying to ignore management revolutions and assuming they have no impact on a project – or conversely letting the organisational changes become the sole focus of attention so project progress grinds to a halt

Changing *sponsors* and *stakeholders* with differing needs and interests in the project

Uncertainty of outcomes

Projects becoming focal points of political battles

The guide

Revolutions and counter-revolutions are central and often repeated parts of history. They stretch into the current times, and will no doubt continue to happen in future. Revolutions pitch one group with existing powers against another group who want to seize power. The stakes are usually high for both sides.

However, let us not spend too much time thinking about the revolutionaries or those currently in power. Instead we need to focus on the rest of society. Those trying to maintain their grasp on power and the revolutionaries are often relatively small groups of people. The majority of society is made up of nervous onlookers with their own hopes and fears. The onlookers are deciding if and when to get actively involved. Too early and too obvious support for a nascent new regime can be fatal – but so can too slow or too long obedience to the old. The general public risk being labelled as betraying revolutionaries or traitorous reactionaries by either side. Most people just want to get on with their lives.

So what has this to do with projects? Well, thankfully, projects are usually not the scene of real revolutions with firing squads and literal battles. But organisations are inherently political, and with any political situation there are ongoing tussles over power and regime changes – albeit just management regime changes, when one group of senior managers tries to replace another. The analogy of the revolution is apt, not because one side replaces the other, but because revolutions are typified by a period of uncertainty when it is unclear which side is going to win out.

Such periods of uncertainty can be a nightmare for projects and project managers. The most obvious effects can be in terms of assessing direction and whether the project is still aligned with it, and getting decisions made. Who makes key decisions when the management hierarchy is in flux? Will the new regime continue to support the project? The situation often creates a sense of malaise in project teams – people take their foot off the pedal whilst the uncertainty is ongoing. At best projects slow down, at worst they effectively stop.

Dealing with the situation

So what can you do as a project sponsor or manager? There is no fixed set of rules or standard set of foolproof instructions that will cover every situation. These are often times for careful and nimble footwork from the project sponsor and manager. Being affected by company politics is usually unavoidable – but there are some things you can do.

First of all, the most important thing is to focus in on the project team. Keep everyone engaged in the job in hand. Avoid long gossip sessions when people predict who are going to be the management winners and losers. The work still needs to be done, the plan still needs to be followed, deliverables should be produced and outcomes achieved. Most people's daily job on the project can carry on. Keep reminding the team of this, and keep managing them so they keep working. For most people, giving some certainty and direction in a time of flux is calming and motivational.

The next thing you should try to do is to avoid your project being at the very heart of the revolution. I have been involved in projects which were at the centre of management shake-ups and it is an unpleasant and non-productive place to be. This may be out of your control. But the way you position or talk about your project certainly influences the level of management focus on a project. In a revolution, being an unobserved and yet essential part of society is often the best place to be.

Thirdly, let your stakeholders know that the management turbulence is having an impact on delivery. This will not necessarily stop the politics going on, but stressing to your leaders that whatever is happening needs to be brought to a close, helps them to realise that things need to progress to a conclusion quickly. There is a cost to disruption. Leaders need to take responsibility for that cost. Projects thrive in environments of certainty and stability. We never have perfect certainty and stability – but the closer we can get to it the better.

Fourthly, try to avoid getting directly involved in the politics yourself, unless you really know what you are doing. Most of us cannot predict, reliably, the outcome of management power struggles – whatever we may think. In real revolutions people are often forced to choose sides. In organisations life is easier, and it is normally possible to sit on the sidelines and wait for the outcome. If you play politics and get it wrong, it can be bad news for you and your project. Try to present the project as something that is good for the organisation irrespective of who is in charge. Provide clear and consistent information to anyone who asks for it, and try to keep your project team independent of any one side in the battles.

Finally, keep confirming the relevance of the project to the changing environment. The project manager and the project sponsor must reflect on the *objectives, scope* and requirements of the project. Normally, these were determined before the management revolution. As the revolution unfolds are they still relevant? Do they need to be modified? Can they be adapted? Whilst it is always painful to stop a project that is partially complete, it is better to do this than keep using resources on something no-one now wants.

Playing poker

One colleague of mine, in a particularly political situation, compared managing projects in these situations to playing poker. You have to decide when to play, when to hold and when to fold. At times you have to become a poker player observing what is going on in the management battles – deciding when to keep the project going full steam ahead, when to slow down and monitor the situation, and hopefully, only very occasionally, when to fold.

Project manager's checklist

■ Focus on the project team even more than usual. Give them as much certainty and clear direction as possible

- Avoid the project becoming a central part of the management revolution

- Let leaders and stakeholders know the impact of the turbulence on the project

- Avoid direct engagement in the politics

- Confirm the relevance of the project to the changing environment. If necessary adapt or cease the project

case study

When everything is changing

Mary is a specialist in organisational transformations. She is involved in reshaping organisations to meet future challenges. She describes her core competency as based on a combination of project *and* change management *skills. She shares some experiences of working on change projects.*

'The initiatives I'm involved in bring about large-scale change to organisations, and as a result tend to affect the people in the project team beyond the simple fact that they are working on the project. Individuals working on a change project are not only trying to deliver change, they are impacted directly by the change themselves. Sometimes the projects are occurring in tough situations, such as businesses which must radically reduce their costs to stay in business. In such situations, even the roles of the initiating sponsors and senior stakeholders can be affected by the project.

'This can make such initiatives very political, unstable, uncertain and subject to ongoing modification in scope, approach, objectives and stakeholders. You have to be very resilient and flexible to work in such environments.

'I see my role in running such projects as trying to give the project team a space in which they can successfully work. Whilst there may be ongoing change and uncertainty, I can't constantly adapt what the project team must do or else they would never get anything done. I am a buffer and a filter.

> 'As a buffer I try to protect the team from everything going on around them. As a filter I try to cut through all the different information, communications and rumours which circulate in such situations. I want the team to know everything they need to know, but not to get bogged down in every detail and every rumour, much of which is irrelevant to their work.'

The improving project manager

There are no perfect project managers. There is always more to learn: about the discipline itself, about the environments in which you operate, or about the disciplines in interfaces as we discussed in Part 7. Additionally, project management is at heart about people management – it is people who deliver projects and not project management itself. We can all, always, learn more about dealing with other people!

There are certain personality traits that make some people naturally good project managers, whilst others will tend to struggle. But project management is not rocket science, and anyone with the right attitude and aptitude can learn to be a good project manager.

The best project managers do not treat what they know as a static and never-changing body of knowledge. They seek to learn more, and impart more knowledge to their project teams. This part deals with the topics of learning and improving in a project management context.

The first section looks at learning in general from projects. The second section explores some of the opportunities, and pitfalls, of seeking best practices and continuous improvement. The next section describes the specific challenges of changing from one style of project management to another, as typified by the move from waterfall to agile lifecycles. The final section discusses building a delivery capability.

Learning from projects

What is this about and why is it important?

Projects are fantastic opportunities to learn. Each project is different from every other project: in terms of the task, the team or the context. Each project brings new challenges to project teams. This environment of challenge encourages development and offers learning opportunities. Whilst each project is unique, there is sufficient commonality between projects for valuable lessons to be learned and widely applied.

The best lessons for *project management* come from live projects. Project management is a practical discipline – and is best developed and improved from practical experience. Sitting in a room and thinking about project management is never as effective as observing and working with project teams and finding out what really works and what does not.

The track record in learning from projects is patchy. Some organisations are successful at learning, and project delivery improves all the time: many are not. The same old problems occur again and again. Successes in one project are not reflected in other projects. Organisations that are most successful at project delivery reach out and learn from projects.

Objectives

- To utilise projects effectively as learning opportunities
- To apply lessons at an individual and an organisational level

➤ Limited engagement in the opportunity to learn from projects

➤ Going through the motions of project reviews, with no active drive to apply the lessons

➤ Culture that does not support learning

The guide

This section deals with learning and development from projects. Each of us naturally learns from our experiences as we go along. I do not want to focus on this individual *ad hoc* learning which happens anyway. I want to focus on optimising the learning opportunity, at an individual and organisational level.

The most effective learning takes place when we take the time to review the experience of doing something, to reflect on it, to discuss it and to consider what was good and should be encouraged, as well as what was less successful and needs improvement.

Project reviews

Every mature project management approach includes the concept of an end-of-project review. These are usually formal sessions when the team gets together to review what can be learned from the project. The process is well understood, but often poorly implemented.

Key lessons for well-implemented project reviews include:

■ **Hold them(!):** it is obvious, but the biggest problem is that teams do not hold the review session. Do not ignore reviews and just jump onto the next project. The investment in time is worth it.

■ **Get the timing right:** hold reviews soon after a project is complete so knowledge is fresh, but not the very next day as some lessons will take a few days to emerge.

■ **Think about good as well as bad:** do not just focus on what went wrong. Focus on the good things too. It is often much more effective to do more of what a team is good at than try to fix every problem.

■ **Consider the whole project:** there is a tendency to focus on the most recent, which in a project review is the end of the project. But there are lessons from every stage of a project.

■ **Be action and commitment orientated:** a review is only of value if it results in changes in behaviour. No change in behaviour – nothing has been learned. Lessons learned should be backed by tangible actions committed to by named individuals.

■ **Outcome as well as process learning:** project management processes and tools can be improved in project reviews, but so can the way deliverables were created and outcomes were achieved. Think about all the dimensions of a project.

Building a learning environment

One of the reasons that project reviews are poorly adhered to is that there is no learning environment in the organisation. As a project manager I always want to hold a review so I and the team can reflect and learn. But extending this learning beyond the team requires a willingness in an organisation to apply lessons. It needs a culture which values learning.

Organisations can build an 'infrastructure' which supports learning. Examples include: document libraries where materials can be found and re-used; widespread and open communication of good practices from projects; and the provision of coaches to facilitate and encourage learning.

A focus purely on learning infrastructure is not enough. Whether an organisation learns or not is deeply ingrained in the culture of the organisation. This is more complex than a few lines can encompass. But some questions can help to identify organisations in which learning thrives. Such organisations answer 'yes' to the following types of questions:

- Are individuals allocated to project teams to learn as well as for effective project delivery?
- Is learning considered an important benefit from every project?
- Are individuals empowered to take actions and implement the lessons learned?
- Does knowledge capture and exploitation receive encouragement, positive feedback or reward?
- When projects are complete do senior *stakeholders* ask – what did we learn, how do we apply this learning?
- Do individuals come forward to take ownership for resolving wider issues that projects throw up?

From learning to continuous improvement

If an organisation develops a learning environment it encourages continuous improvement. But one specific problem with learning on projects is the way project reviews are thought of. Project reviews are important, but they are often seen as the *only* learning opportunity on projects. A more effective approach to take is to encourage learning throughout the life of the project.

This is one thing I like about good implementations of *agile*. The approach agile takes to learning can be applied to other project management styles, even a totally *waterfall* project can benefit. There are two aspects: the removal of impediments and the retrospective.

Agile works to remove impediments by building their resolution into iteration *backlog* and learning from the process. Additionally, every *sprint* in an agile project – typically a 2–4 week iteration of work – should be followed by a retrospective. A retrospective is a review, but instead of being a one off, it is a regularly repeated session in projects. The frequency of such reviews significantly improves learning.

Occasionally, you find a critical issue or opportunity that makes a dramatic improvement in performance, but in reality most improvements are incremental. The lesson from approaches such as *lean, six sigma* and coaching in sport, shows that those organisations which succeed continually apply incremental improvements. They regularly reflect and apply what they learn and seek continuous improvement. Projects are ideal environments to apply continuous improvements.

From individual learning to organisational learning

It is great when individuals learn from projects and better when the teams learn. Best of all is when the whole organisation can learn from each project. This requires the effective communication of appropriate lessons from individual projects to the wider organisation. This is most effectively achieved when there is an individual or team who have responsibility for spreading the lessons from successful and unsuccessful projects. Such teams should resist the temptation of trying to teach everyone every lesson, as this just drowns people in information. A better approach is to periodically update people with great ideas that they can apply.

There is one important category of issue that offers the opportunity for wider learning: *systemic issues*. Systemic issues are organisation-wide issues which impacted the project and will impact others, for example, problems with resource allocation, decision making or prioritisation.

Project teams will often identify out-of-*scope* systemic problems. The difficulty is that the team usually cannot resolve them and do not know who to pass them on to. This is an opening for *portfolio management* teams to add huge value by taking ownership for such issues and to work to resolve them for the wider benefit of the organisation.

Project manager's checklist

- Projects offer ideal opportunities for learning
- Project reviews are a good way to learn from projects – as long as they result in action

■ End-of-project reviews should not be regarded as the only learning opportunity. The most effective learning occurs when there are regular times to review, reflect and discuss the project

■ The most valuable learning takes place when an organisation's culture values learning and spreads the knowledge from individual projects to the wider organisation

Best practice, continuous improvement and accreditation

What is this about and why is it important?

Successful project delivery is critically important in many organisations. The difference in performance between the most and least effective project teams is huge. Some organisations have many highly effective project teams. Others struggle repeatedly with poor project performance and, as a result, seek improvement.

There are different ways to improve *project management* performance: adopt best practices, instigate continuous improvement, seek accreditation or benchmark *maturity levels*. Each way can lead to increased performance, but often fails to achieve expected improvements.

This section reviews best practice, continuous improvement and accreditation as sources of improved project management. The next section builds on this by discussing practical ways to implement new project management approaches. (This section also relates to pp. 136 and 231.)

Objectives

- To understand the benefits and pitfalls of project management best practice, continuous improvement and accreditation
- To build the basis to optimise project management performance

┌─ **Common issues in achieving these objectives**
├─► Uncritical acceptance of claimed best practices
├─► Using the language of continuous improvement without making regular changes
└─► Focusing on project management accreditation or maturity levels as a goal, rather than a means to improvement

The guide

Best practice

A phrase often thrown around in conversations about project management is 'best practice'. This phrase is not unique to project management, but is popular within the project management community.

Let us consider typical examples of people using this phrase. During project reviews, it may be used to justify an approach: 'Why are we doing it that way – well, it's best practice.' The other time is when consultants and service providers sell their products. They regularly claim they use best practice. We should applaud anyone who knows the best way. If it is the best way, we should all be doing it.

However, there are problems with this thinking. Firstly, many of the proponents of best practice present it as scientifically researched, unchallengeable, infallible wisdom. But most of these proponents are self-pronounced experts. They are trying to be helpful, but most so-called best practice is nothing more than what they have found works well on the projects they have worked on. There is nothing intrinsically wrong with that – we can learn and improve from others' experience. But what I've found works in the past is not the same as proven best practice.

An appealing thought is to do more research to find the true best practices. I remain sceptical. Underlying the words best practice is an implied *assumption* that there actually can be such a thing as best practice. My scepticism comes from my belief that every project is unique, it works in a distinct context, has a specific team and its own goals. What is best in one situation is not necessarily best in another.

Of course tools, techniques, practices and processes should be re-used. There is sufficient similarity between many projects that common approaches can be applied. This is the basis of the discipline of project management. But we should be cautious in thinking of anything labelled as best practice as truly universal best practice. At most it is best practice in some situations.

This leads to the other worry I have with best practice. If something really is best, then it cannot be improved. If it could it was never best practice in the first place. But nothing really is the best forever – what is the best practice today may be irrelevant in a few years' time.

Am I against all the things labelled as best practice? No. I prefer inexperienced teams using weak project management disciplines to adopt 'best practice', whatever the real truth of its status as best. However, experienced senior project teams should review the practices available, try and understand the mindset behind the variants of best practice, and select what is optimal for that situation. By all means adopt things called best practice, but do not fool yourself that it really is the best or that you cannot improve on it.

Continuous improvement

What is the alternative to everyone accepting best practice as a given? The answer lies in the adoption of a continuous improvement mentality to our project management practices. Start with whatever is best practice in your specific project management domain, then improve it.

The words 'continuous improvement' are easy to say, but few people put them into active practice. We all learn from each and every project we do, but few of us truly go back to our tools, techniques, processes or templates during every project and consider what can be improved and developed. Whatever the hype, few organisations I have dealt with are good at continuous improvement in project management. Continuous improvement is a mindset, a set of behaviours and a culture. It cannot be achieved simply by saying the words repeatedly!

However, even though I am a fan, I have concerns with continuous improvement. I do come across the other extreme, where continuous improvement is itself a fixed mantra. There are two problems with the over-zealous application of the concept of continuous improvement:

1 It becomes an excuse to do things half-heartedly, as in 'Don't worry, we can always improve on it'.

2 It creates confusion for team members. We need some stability as we take time to learn new things. If all processes are being adapted continuously, no-one knows if what they are doing is the right way or if they are following the latest standard. This then points to some sort of *change control* or release management over our tools, processes and so on. But unfortunately, the words 'change control' often seem anathema to many of the staunchest advocates of continuous improvement.

Accreditation and maturity levels

Another approach to improved project management performance is to seek accreditation for project managers and key project team members such as those working in a *project management office (PMO)*. This may be achieved by investing in training followed by the necessary exams, or by only recruiting formally qualified project managers.

Such individual accreditation can be very useful. It provides a minimum standard of common knowledge across a project management community. *Sponsors* and customers can have an expectation of a level of knowledge in all project teams. A powerful side-effect is that standard accreditation provides a common language which is very helpful.

However, project management is a practical discipline. Like most practical disciplines you learn by doing much more than you will ever learn in a classroom. Reflection and review are powerful, reading and researching add value, classroom training is helpful – but it is practical experience of success and failure in project management that teaches you most.

Additionally, too many of the most popular courses are taught by rote by trainers with limited current project management experience. In the worst examples, project managers sit through hours of PowerPoint decks and then cram for an exam, which they promptly forget. Good training is interactive and builds on the experiences of the trainer and the trainees, and the focus is primarily on the learning not the qualification. The quality of the person giving the training is as important as the slide decks used in training.

In addition to accreditation at an individual level, it is possible to seek accreditation at an organisational level. One way to achieve this is through maturity levels. The concept of maturity levels developed in the software industry by the CMMI Institute but has spread to other disciplines including project management. A maturity level is a defined set of practices, processes and behaviours an organisation consistently applies to produce expected outcomes. The Association for Project Management (*APM*) developed the *P3M3* model, and the Project Management Institute (*PMI*) have the *OPM3* model.

Benchmarking maturity levels is instructive and helpful. Seeking to improve maturity levels appropriately can drive performance improvements in project teams, and help in achieving standardisation.

High maturity may be desirable, but the highest maturity levels are not achieved for free, and you may not need to be at the highest levels. If you seek a high level, make sure in complying with all requirements you are not over-engineering your project management approach. Additionally, compliance checking will be required, and this should not be overly onerous.

With all forms of individual or organisational accreditation the aim must be to improve project success – if not, the investment is worthless.

Project manager's checklist

- There are multiple sources of ideas to improve project performance: adopt best practices, instigate continuous improvement, seek accreditation or benchmark maturity levels

- Each can significantly improve project performance, if applied in the right way as a means to improvement

- But each has pitfalls. When they become goals in their own rights, they tend to add overhead without commensurate benefits

Adopting a new project management approach

What is this about and why is it important?

The last section looked at the sources of enhancements to an organisation's *project management* capability. This section builds on this, by discussing the challenges with implementing such enhancements.

This section is relevant in four situations: enhancing or updating an existing approach; implementing a standard project management approach where multiple approaches have previously been used; changing project management approach, for example from *critical path* to *critical chain*, or *waterfall* to *agile*; and implementing a formal project management approach for the first time.

Objectives

- To understand the challenges in implementing a new project management approach
- To take advantage of advances in project management

Common issues in achieving these objectives

- Insufficient understanding or analysis of the root causes of delivery problems
- Underestimating the degree of change that adopting a new approach entails

The guide

Solving the right problem

Organisations are often dissatisfied with their delivery performance. When this occurs there is a tendency to look for ways to improve project management. Before starting to implement enhanced project management, you should be confident that the problem lies with project management.

Even the best project management approach will not solve all delivery problems. Many common delivery issues relate to the environment in which projects run, for example: resourcing, prioritisation, the stability of strategies, decision making, and the relationship between project and operational work (see pp. 73, 136, 148 and 154). These wider management issues can be resolved, or at least their effects mitigated, but the solution does not lie purely in the project management domain.

Additionally, the way an organisation delivers projects may be based on good and appropriate practice and the problem lies with unrealistic expectations. Projects really may require more time and cost than an organisation wants, and the *risks* a project is exposed to can become reality! Good project management can help in setting realistic expectations, but only when the *stakeholder* community listens.

Another issue lies with the capability of project staff. Poor project performance may be a reflection of untrained, inexperienced or low-capability project teams. A robust project management approach can help to steer inexperienced or lower-capability teams, but it will not solve all problems. Investing in coaching, training or recruiting more experienced staff may be a more effective solution.

The willingness to change

Project management is dynamic. There are always refinements and enhancements. But whilst the discipline moves on, there are project managers applying the same approach they applied years or even decades ago, as if they work in a static discipline. Perhaps this is because we do not like to fiddle with things we know work. Yet to gain the most from project management there must be a willingness to adapt and change as the discipline evolves.

My story with regard to one of the hot topics of project management over the past few years – agile – is probably typical. Coming from a traditional waterfall-style project background, albeit with forays into various *iterative* projects and accepting the premise of *progressive elaboration*, I was sceptical of agile. I knew the problems of waterfall, but had also been involved in many successful waterfall projects.

Agile sounded like a pipedream. I heard and believed the myths: there is no process, it is no good for big projects and so on. Fortunately, I got the chance to work with some great agile teams. There is no better teacher than experience, and once I got to work with agile teams who really knew what they were doing I was quickly convinced.

Yet even though I am now a fan of agile, it is just another tool. A good tool, that is powerful in some situations, but is not without flaws and dependencies on human behaviour. It works in environments which support it, and with projects of the right characteristics to benefit from it. On the other hand, you do not need to implement every aspect of agile to gain benefits from it – techniques like daily stand-ups and regular retrospectives can be productive in many project environments.

But how quickly the revolutionaries become reactionaries! Agile was developed in the software industry to overcome challenges with traditional project approaches, after realising there was a better way. It is therefore ironic that some of the most rigid project people are the agile zealots who insist on absolutely rigid adherence to some specific variant of agile. This risks taking a brilliant set of insights and making the next bit of yesterday's news.

There is something very human about this attitude. We need to push ourselves to accept that whatever we hold close to our hearts may not be the best. At most it is just the best we have for the time being.

Adopt what seems best, but be willing to go further. Project management, by itself, is not the answer to anything. It is a powerful tool. Like the best of tools it needs to be applied in the right way to the right situation. And we, like the best toolmakers, should always be looking to improve on that toolset.

The right project management approach

In selecting the right approach, be realistic. No solution is a silver bullet to every single project management problem. The approach is a tool, not the answer in itself (see p. 154). The right solution should be appropriate for your specific needs, but by itself will not solve your problems.

There is a tendency to get over-excited by the design of project management processes, tools and practices. With this excitement comes a risk of excessive complexity. But if something is so complex that you cannot explain it quickly and simply, it is probably not implementable no matter how good it is.

Your new approach has to be usable by the target project management community. This depends on skill levels, capabilities and experience. Often a simple solution achieves as much as a theoretically richer solution, because the target users do not have the ability to understand or utilise the richness of the fuller solution. There is no point offering novices a highly complex, very mature solution.

A solution tends to imply a level of standardisation. There is great value in standardisation. When everyone uses the same concepts then situations become clearer, and measurement and control become simpler. But beware of enforcing a one size fits all approach, unless all your projects are similar. Situations vary and you may need multiple approaches. For example, it is possible for agile and waterfall to coexist in one organisation. What is often more important than a single project management approach is a common approach to *quality management* and *governance*.

Implementing the new solution

You could be adopting formal project management for the first time, applying a new project management way of thinking, enhancing some practices, improving the project management environment such as implementing a new planning tool, or adopting *programme* or *portfolio management*. Whichever it is, changing a project management approach is a change project in its own right that needs planning and control and which has risks.

How do you implement such changes? There are two extremes, between which most enhancements sit. Such changes may be:

1 **Pushed out from a centre:** typically achieved by writing a standard in a manual, providing training and then mandating use of the defined standard.

2 **Pulled by practitioners:** the voluntary and proactive adoption of new approaches by practitioners.

I am wary of push-only approaches. Experience in *change management* indicates that the most successful changes have an element of pull from the user community – ideally a strong element. If this does not exist in the first place it needs to be encouraged by explaining the new approach to everyone so they can see the benefits. However, some degree of central consolidation, control and standardisation is also important.

Irrespective of push or pull, good communications, training, coaching and alignment with performance management processes are essential. In fact, all the elements of a successful change project are required. To achieve a successful implementation the affected community must understand the new approach, have the capability to use it, be willing to use it, and have access to support during the transition phase.

The project management approach does not work in isolation. Other aspects such as the *quality assurance* (QA) and *quality control* (QC) of projects (see p. 122), governance and resourcing processes may also need to be updated and aligned with the new approach.

Finally, consideration should be given to how staff are encouraged to adopt and maintain adherence to the new approach, and how continuous development will be encouraged and controlled (see p. 231).

Project manager's checklist

■ Enhanced project management approaches can improve delivery performance – but will not, alone, resolve delivery problems caused by unrealistic expectations, unskilled project teams or a poor project environment

■ To ensure high delivery performance there must be a willingness to change, and to continue to change as project management approaches evolve

■ No single approach is right for every situation; you must select the right approach for your unique context

■ Implementing a new project management approach is a change project in its own right

Building a project delivery capability

What is this about and why is it important?

This book has journeyed through a range of discussions on *project management*, with the aim of helping to improve either your own or your organisation's project management capability. But there is a bigger picture to be drawn in which project management is just one component. I call this a *delivery capability*.

A (project) delivery capability is the complete set of assets an organisation needs to be able to reliably deliver projects – of which project management is one key component. In a short section like this it is not possible to go into every aspect of a delivery capability, but I want to end this book by giving a flavour of the main components. I do this to set project management in context, being a firm believer that for many organisations their delivery capability is as important as their strategic or operational capabilities.

Objectives

- To highlight the importance of a project delivery capability
- To give a picture of a holistic delivery capability and help in developing one

Common issues in achieving these objectives

The relatively low regard given to delivery compared to other critical organisational activities such as strategy development, sales and marketing, and operations

Lack of willingness or ability to design and implement a complete delivery capability

The guide

From projects to delivery

This book has discussed projects as individual items. But it is rarely a case of doing one project and then forgetting about it. For most organisations there is a continuous stream of projects. To some extent, managing streams of projects are the concerns of *programme* and *portfolio management*, but building a true delivery capability is much broader than this.

To deliver projects reliably and repeatedly needs more than good project management: it needs a complete delivery capability. A delivery capability is complex, but the primary building blocks are relatively simple:

- the human resources to deliver projects;
- a supportive management culture and behaviours;
- a flexible organisational architecture;
- the supporting tools, techniques, processes, practices and methodologies;
- mechanisms to continually grow and improve the delivery capability.

Let us look at each of these in turn.

Human resources

The most important factor determining whether an organisation reliably delivers is the availability of capable, motivated people to do the work. The most obvious people are project managers, but project managers do not do all the work on projects. A project takes a range of people to create the deliverables, make change happen, achieve outcomes and deliver business benefits.

This may seem obvious, but frequently I come across the situation in which the solution to every need to deliver a project is simply to allocate a project manager. Project managers are important – but if they are not supported by the other resources required, then the project cannot be done or the rest of the staff in an organisation have to multi-task on more and more projects. Both are inefficient, and often ineffective.

The delivery environment

The next critical factor determining an organisation's degree of success in delivering projects is what I call the *delivery environment*. The delivery environment is made up a series of critical but often relatively intangible aspects: organisational culture, management behaviour and how project teams are encouraged and rewarded (p. 136 discusses this in more detail).

Perhaps because much of it is intangible, few organisations deliberately work to develop the most productive delivery environment. Yet I cannot stress how important this is, and how much difference it makes to project delivery.

Examples of aspects of this delivery environment include:

- how strategy and idea generation feeds into project, programme and portfolio management;
- how decisions are made;
- how effective and clear prioritisation is;
- how resources are allocated to projects, and the quality of those resources;
- the way deliverables typically transition from projects to in-life operations;
- the support and sponsorship senior managers and executives give to projects;
- the capabilities of senior managers to productively support projects;
- how *systemic issues* are dealt with.

The organisation's architecture

The next feature I consider as part of the delivery capability is the architecture of the organisation. I use this term in a very broad sense to include products and services, organisational structures, systems, processes, policies, facilities, tools, roles and responsibilities and other assets used in running the business. The end result of every project is to change some part of this architecture – if nothing changes then a project delivers no benefit.

There are some organisations which have been designed, or more usually not designed at all but simply evolved, in such a way that making any change is difficult. There are other organisations in which changes are comparatively simple. The underlying difference comes down to flexibility and adaptability to change of the organisational architecture – enabling project success by making something better, faster or cheaper.

Organisations can be architected or designed with flexibility in mind. Usually, it is not a matter of making everything flexible and easy to change, but identifying the parts of the organisational architecture that are regularly changed by projects or which get in the way of delivery. These are then designed and developed to be as flexible and adaptable as possible.

Tools, techniques, processes, practices and methodologies of project management

The next features are those aspects which have been discussed throughout this book. The project management practices, processes, tools, techniques and methodologies. As an advocate of project management I believe these are important, add value and significantly enhance delivery capability. However, without the previous features being in place they will always be limited in impact.

Project management works best when it is aligned with the supporting capabilities required to deliver in an organisation. These vary from organisation to organisation, but typically include capabilities such as *change management* and business analysis.

There should be clear links between delivery and the other key components of an organisation. The delivery capability sits between strategy and operations. Delivery takes the ideas from strategy and makes them the operational reality of the business.

This requires the development of strategies that are deliverable by your delivery capability, and environments in which delivery teams appreciate operational realities and can successfully and smoothly transition from projects to operations.

Improving the delivery capability

Building a delivery capability is just like developing any other capability in an organisation. No-one nowadays expects to implement the perfect operational capability that never changes or is never enhanced. Change and enhancement are ingrained into operational management practice with concepts and techniques such as the Deming cycle, total *quality management*, statistical process control, continuous improvement, *lean* and *six sigma*. A great delivery capability is also subject to development and continuous improvement.

A competitive differentiator?

Organisation leaders tend not to focus on project management – they are more interested in strategies, sales and marketing, and operations. Yet this misses an important opportunity. Because behind all of these is an ability to execute ideas and turn them into reliable operational capabilities. And a core element of execution is project management and the wider concept of a delivery capability.

Strategies and ideas come and go, whilst competencies and capabilities are more deeply ingrained into organisations. It is possible to have a distinctive and better project management capability than your competitors. There are many examples, across sectors, of businesses that thrive because they can deliver more quickly, cheaply and reliably than competitors.

A core competency is something that adds value and is not easily copied. On paper a great project management capability should be easy to copy: just implement a few processes and hire a few experienced project managers. In practice, building a reliable and sustainable delivery capability is not trivial, but once achieved is a valuable and hard to copy asset for an organisation.

Project manager's checklist

- Project management is part of a wider delivery capability which determines an organisation's success in delivering projects

- There are several components to this delivery capability which tend to develop in an *ad hoc* fashion, but can be deliberately designed and improved to maximise project success

- Such a delivery capability can be the sources of competitive differentiation

Building a project management team

Martin is currently the Programme Director for a manufacturing company. In this role he has defined the need for and set up a central team of project and programme managers to deliver the major initiatives in the organisation. He has significant experience of setting up project management competency centres and rolling out project management methodologies.

'I've started up and built several project teams. This involves shaping roles, recruiting people and converting the business to a new way of working – as inevitably if there was no project team, then historically projects were not always done in the most structured manner.

'I've got strong views of the right and wrong way of delivering projects. But, I've also learned that I have to be willing to try new things as there is no one size fits all approach to project management. It depends on the type of projects, the context and the culture of the organisation. However, when I work to set up a new project team I do need a clear vision of where I'm going.

'The clear vision is needed for the simple practical reason that without it I won't end up where I want to be. There is a political dimension as well. New team members look to a team leader to have a clear vision as it gives them confidence and a sense of direction.

'However, irrespective of the precise role, size and approach of the project management teams I have set up I always insist on two things.

First of all, I insist that the best people the organisation can afford are recruited, and do not accept the project team as a dumping ground for anyone who just feels like being a project manager. I'm more than willing to take on inexperienced people and help them develop their skills – but they must have potential and the right attitude. Secondly, I am consistent in setting the expectation that the project team will do the highest quality of work, and anyone who does not want to do this should not come into the team.

'The building and recruiting of team members can be a long-winded task. But more difficult still is building an approach to projects across the organisation that is followed. It is not just the project managers who need to follow this approach, everyone involved in projects do. Don't under-estimate the effort and time it takes to really implement a high standard of project management across an organisation – it's usually a major change initiative in its own right.'

Glossary

This glossary contains definitions of the key project management terminology used in this book. All definitions are the author's own. The terms are defined as they are used in project management contexts.

Agile An innovative style of *project management* that evolved, and continues to evolve, from the *Manifesto for Agile Software Development*, written in 2001. Initially a software development approach, and using a number of software specific techniques such as pair programming and continuous integration, the agile approach is being adapted and applied increasingly to non-software development projects.

APM Acronym for the Association of Project Management.

Assumption A proposition taken as true in the absence of known facts. In projects there are usually many assumptions.

Assumption management The practice of identifying, assessing the risk associated with, tracking and responding to changes in *assumptions*. It closely links to *risk management*.

Backlog A prioritised list of activities to be addressed in a *sprint* within an *agile* project.

Baseline plan/re-baselined An agreed plan which presents the expected way a project will progress. This is usually agreed by the project manager with the project *sponsor* and other *stakeholders*.

A plan is re-baselined or updated, with the approval of the project sponsor and key stakeholders when reality is at significant variance with the baseline plan. The updates are subject to *change control* and as a plan is re-baselined it is usually formally version controlled.

Benefits realisation The practice of managing the achievement of benefits from a project.

Benefits tracking The practice of regularly assessing the benefits achieved by a project. By tracking benefits the project team and project *stakeholders* can assess how well a project is progressing towards achieving the project's business case.

Body of knowledge (BoK) A complete set of practices, *lifecycles*, processes and terminology making up *project management*, as recognised and defined by various project management associations. The most well known are the PM BoK from the *PMI*, and the APM BoK from the *APM*.

Change control A formal process used to ensure that changes to agreed *project management* parameters and definitions (*scope*, *objectives*, plans, etc.) are introduced in a controlled and co-ordinated manner.

Change management A professional discipline and *body of knowledge* dealing with the introduction of changes, for example as a result of a project, into organisations. Change management focuses predominantly on the human aspect of change.

Change request A formal request to alter some aspect of a project – for example requirements, *objectives, scope*, etc. The request is assessed and managed through the *change control* process.

Critical chain A *project management* approach based on the work of Eliyahu Goldratt and the Theory of Constraints, determining the critical activities (or chain) within a project that a project manager should focus on. It is an alternative to *critical path* project management.

Critical path The series of activities (or path) in a project plan, which, when interdependencies are considered, determines the duration of the project.

Decomposition The practice of breaking down aspects of a project (e.g. activities or deliverables) into smaller components to aid understanding, planning, monitoring and control.

Delivery capability The capability within an organisation to deliver projects and *programmes*.

Delivery environment The environment within an organisation in which projects take place. The delivery environment includes factors such as culture, attitude to projects, resource levels and capabilities. Depending on the delivery environment projects may be harder or easier to deliver.

Governance The management framework within which project decision makers are appointed, responsibilities are allocated and decisions are made.

Iterative A style of *project management* in which the *lifecycle* is repeated in a cyclical fashion, improving the deliverables created after each iteration of the lifecycle until mature deliverables are produced. Unlike *waterfall,* iterative lifecycles encourage enhancement in requirements and learning about customer needs as the project progresses. The customers can review the deliverables after each iteration and determine how closely they fit their needs.

Jira A software product, created and marketed by Atlassian, used extensively in *agile* projects for managing project *backlogs*.

Kanban A work scheduling system, originally used in *lean* and just-in-time manufacturing but now being adopted by some lightweight versions of *agile*.

Lean A form of *project management* based on the lean principles used widely in manufacturing. Lean is often associated with *agile* projects. Lean is focused on value as perceived by the customer and eliminating all non-value-adding tasks.

Lifecycle A logical sequence of activities to accomplish a project's objectives or outcome. There are many different lifecycles – for example *waterfall* or *iterative*.

Maturity level/P3M3/OPM3 A defined stage in a maturity model. Maturity models describe the capabilities an organisation should have to achieve mature *project management*. Organisations can be assessed and formally graded to a specific level on a maturity model.

There are different maturity models for project management – for example the *PMI's* OPM3 and Office of Government Commerce's P3M3.

MECE Acronym for mutually exclusive, cumulatively exhaustive.

MS Project A widespread project planning and management tool from Microsoft.

Objectives The high-level definition of why a project is to be undertaken, related to the business benefits an organisation should reap from investing in a project.

Opportunities A positive *risk* – that is an uncertain future event that if realised will cause the project outcome to be better than currently expected. By identifying opportunities project teams can determine ways of increasing the probability and impact of opportunities hence increasing the overall likelihood of project success.

Planning poker A participative practice, often used in *agile* projects, for estimating the length of various aspects of the project (in agile based on *stories*). Planning poker aims to achieve consensus in the team about the size of the work required to deliver the project.

PMI Acronym for the Project Management Institute.

Portfolio A set of projects using the same pool of resources, usually the set of projects being pursued by an organisation.

Portfolio management Portfolio management is the centralised management of the *portfolio* – for example prioritising between projects, resource management across projects, etc.

PRINCE 2 A common process-based methodology originally developed by the Office of Government Commerce for public sector projects, but widely used in the private sector.

It is also commonly used as short-hand amongst project managers to refer to certification to PRINCE 2 standards (at foundation or practitioner level).

Programme (US program) There are multiple definitions of programmes, but the most useful is to consider a programme as a related set of projects with common objective(s).

Programme management The set of practices, processes and tools used to manage *programmes*. Programme management is related to, but extends upon, *project management* to overcome the specific challenges of programmes.

Programme manager The individual responsible for the successful delivery of a *programme*, using the discipline of *programme management*. The role of the programme manager is analogous to that of a project manager, but is typically more senior and often more focused on achieving change outcomes rather than simply overseeing the creation of deliverables.

Progressive elaboration A project management practice in which the plan is continuously detailed and enhanced as newer and improved information becomes available to the project team as the project progresses.

Project crashing A technique which attempts to reduce the duration of a project, normally by adding more resources.

Project management A set of reusable practices, processes, tools, and methods which support the successful delivery of projects.

(See p. 8 for a fuller discussion.)

Project management office (PMO) A group or department within a project, programme or organisation that specialises in supporting and guiding projects. PMOs have different roles in different organisations but usually they either support project managers in specific *project management* tasks such as reporting, planning or *risk management*, or they support the execution of *governance* across projects.

Quality assurance (QA) Activities designed to ensure the project is following the right process.

Quality control (QC) Activities designed to ensure the deliverables or work products produced by the project are fit for purpose (which includes, but is not limited to, *testing*).

Quality management (QM) A variety of activities (including *QA* and *QC)* aimed at ensuring a project's quality in terms of approach and outcome.

Quality plan The documented definition of the approach to *quality management* within a project.

RACI chart The documented definition of who is <u>r</u>esponsible or <u>a</u>ccountable for performing various aspects of a project, and who should be <u>c</u>onsulted or <u>i</u>nformed about the performance of those aspects of the project. This is usually presented in a table which may also be referred to as a RACI matrix.

Risk The effect of uncertainty, unknowns and ambiguities on project *objectives*. Frequently, risks are considered as negative, but it is possible to consider positive risks – also known as *opportunities*.

Risk management The identification, assessment, and management of *risks* with an aim of improving the likelihood of achieving the desired project *objectives*.

Scope The definition of the boundaries of a project – or more colloquially, what's in and what's out.

Scrum One of the most common forms of *agile* project management.

Scrum master A central role in *scrum*. The scrum master works with the project team, and ensures the team is working in the spirit of the scrum approach and helps the team to be effective by removing impediments – that is barriers to progress.

Six sigma A set of management practices and a toolkit, originally developed by Motorola. Six sigma improves the quality of process outputs by identifying and removing the causes of defects and minimising variability.

Sponsor A senior manager or executive in an organisation who is accountable for the achievement of a project's *objectives* and business benefits.

Sprint A phase in a project following *agile* or *scrum*.

Stakeholder An individual or group with an interest in a project. Stakeholders are typically able to influence the projects outcome and/or are impacted by it.

Stakeholder management The practice of identifying, assessing and taking action to ensure the smooth running of a project by creating positive relationships with *stakeholders*.

Steering group/committee An advisory committee usually formed of senior *stakeholders* and experts who provide direction to a project, guidance on key issues affecting a project both to the project manager and project sponsor, and ensuring the project has appropriate *governance*.

Stories (agile) Rather than defining requirements in a traditional form, *agile* stories describe what users of the project's deliverables will do or be able to do once the project is complete. Stories are usually short and written in everyday business language, often taking the form of 'as a user I want to …'.

Systemic issues Common problems within an organisation, affecting the delivery of multiple projects within that organisation, which are usually outside of a project's *scope* or project team's capability to resolve.

Testing The formal investigation of a project's deliverables to ensure they meet requirements and are of sufficient quality. Testing is typically a defined phase of a project.

Waterfall A sequential project management *lifecycle* widely used in many industries, and the basis for many common project methodologies. Waterfall lifecycles typically follow phases such as: planning, mobilisation, analysis, design, development, *testing*, implementation, and review.

Work breakdown structure The structured *decomposition* of a project into smaller components, usually based around the deliverables from the project.

Index